Instant
Storm
Forecasting

Alan Watts

SHERIDAN HOUSE

Other titles by the same author

Instant Weather Forecasting
ISBN 978 1 57409 136 6
Reading the clouds is one of the ways of predicting the
weather and in this guide, 24 cloud photographs, with
detailed explanations, give valuable clues to the weather
patterns to enable the reader to predict changes in the
weather ahead.

Instant Wind Forecasting
ISBN 978 1 57409 143 4
A useful guide for reading weather signs and gauging
what the wind will do, based on reading the clouds and
understanding of how weather patterns emerge. An
invaluable book for all those who work outdoors or
enjoy sports such as sailing, fishing or walking.

The Weather Handbook
ISBN 978 1 57409 081 9
The book's many useful tips and rules-of-thumb,
supplemented by color photos and illustrations, are
based on the latest meteorological advances as well as
centuries-old weather lore.

Weather Wise
ISBN 978 1 57409 266 0
A very accessible guide to weather phenomena for the
outdoors enthusiast, explaining how forthcoming
weather will affect them as well as how to predict what
is coming and assess how severe it will be.

This edition published 2009
by Sheridan House Inc.
145 Palisade Street
Dobbs Ferry, New York 10522
www.sheridanhouse.com

Note: while all reasonable care has been taken in the
publication of this edition, the publisher takes no responsibility
for the use of the methods or products described in the book.

Library of Congress Cataloging-in-Publication Data

Watts, Alan
  Instant storm forecasting / Alan Watts.
     p. cm.
  Includes index.
  ISBN 978-1-57409-277-6 (pbk. : alk. paper)
  1. Severe storms—Forecasting. 2. Weather forecasting. I. Title.
  QC941.W37 2009
  551.55—dc22
                                        2008034615

ISBN 978 1 57409 277 6

Printed in Spain

Contents

Introduction 4

Explanations, abbreviations, conversions 5

1 The world's winds and weather 7

2 Bad weather systems 9

3 Gales and tidal surges 13

4 Wind storms 16

5 Thunderstorms 20

6 Lightning 24

7 Tropical revolving storms 28

8 Tornadoes and waterspouts 32

9 Snowstorms 36

10 Mountain storms 40

11 Avalanches 44

12 Floods 48

13 Deep cold and ice storms 50

14 Falling and mountain winds 54

15 Bad weather winds of the world 56

16 El Niño 58

17 Intense heat 62

Index 64

Introduction

Despite its title, this is not a book which will enable you to accomplish what the met services throughout the world are still struggling to do, that is to instantly forecast when a storm is due. What I hope to achieve is to point out the factors you should consider when the professional forecasters have made predictions about coming bad weather – and sometimes even when they haven't.

Reading this book might remind you to disconnect your TV from its aerial when thunder is first heard. It will suggest what gear you may need when you pack for foreign climes where the weather is very different from what you are used to at home; and advise on what precautions you should take.

The world experiences an amazing range of weather conditions, most of which you can enjoy – but you may encounter some atrocious conditions, even in places that are normally set-fair. My aim is to warn about what conditions you could meet, but I would need many more pages to cover all the vagaries of the world's weather.

Instant Storm Forecasting is a companion volume to the other two books in this series. *Instant Weather Forecasting*, which celebrates its fortieth birthday this year, sets out in tabular form, elements to think about when looking at the clouds and helps the reader to foretell what the weather will do. This is a book for everyone but *Instant Wind Forecasting* is aimed largely aimed at sailors, although other sportsmen have found it useful. *Instant Storm Forecasting* follows the same lines; it describes key factors relating to the differing weather conditions (sometimes in tabular form) and points out things to think about before the world's extreme weather conditions heave in sight. As with its companion volumes, *Instant Storm Forecasting* is well-illustrated with carefully selected photographs.

Travel brochures will usually paint a rosy picture of the place you intend to visit for business or a holiday and so it is good to be forewarned about the possibility that this apparently idyllic venue can be subject to some nasty weather conditions. Your vacation might coincide with one of those occasions. For example, the normally benign Mediterranean Sea is subject to the fall-out of desert storms, usually called scirocco gales, but there are other names. These blow northwards from the North African deserts laden with dust and so perhaps a dust filter might be a useful addition to your luggage. Widespread winds can sometimes carry this (often red) dust into southern Europe. Even the north of England is not immune from the fall-out of such storms. You may come out one morning – especially if there has been light rain – to find that your car is covered in little rings of Saharan dust.

Perhaps you are adventurous and intend to visit the eastern part of Western Australia to escape the northern hemisphere winter. So it is as well to know that during the Australian summer they experience a monsoon with very heavy rain.

The mysterious east is less mysterious than it used to be, but one thing that hasn't changed is the frequency of typhoons, so when is the typhoon season? If you go to the southern United States you may encounter hurricanes. Does your insurance cover the consequences of being caught up in one? The Middle East is now opening up as a tourist area but be aware they have their cyclones too.

These and many other topics I have tried to cover in these pages and so I hope this book will give you something to think about. And, even if you're not planning to jet off anywhere at the present time, you will find some absorbing facts and remarkable photographs to fascinate you.

Alan Watts

Explanations, abbreviations and conversions

This section gives more information about technical terms as well as conversions from one set of units to another.

Air masses These are immense bodies of air that are either warmer or colder than normal. They have warm or cold characteristics right up to the tropopause and they form fronts when they meet. The main source of warm air masses is the semi-permanent anticyclones that exist over the tropical seas. Here air stagnates for long periods and so can acquire the temperature and humidity of the sea below. It is called *maritime Tropical air (mT air)*. Similarly air that stagnates in the Polar anticyclones and is then drawn towards the temperate latitudes is called *maritime Polar air (mP air)*. It is the clash of mP and mT air masses that generates most depressions and their fronts.

Other air masses which are less universal include those directly from the Arctic (NH) or Antarctic (SH). These are often very cold. They are not as cold as, for example, *continental Polar (cP)* which comes from great winter anticyclones such as the Siberian High nor as hot as *continental Tropical (cT)* that may come from desert regions.

The weather you experience can be greatly modified by air masses travelling over land (especially mountainous or hilly land) or over water. Meteorologists detect air masses not by what they look like near the Earth's surface but by their upper characteristics.

Convection is vertical movement of air. Air, when it rises, leads to heap clouds and sometimes to showers but there are corresponding down currents to compensate. Strong convection leads to thunderstorms, downpours and hail-storms.

Humidity has a great bearing on our ability to withstand heat and cold. High humidity restricts the body's ability to lose heat by sweating and so makes tropical latitudes unbearable for those who are used to living in temperate regions. Equally extreme northern (NH or southern SH) regimes can be made more bearable by dry surroundings. High humidity with attendant cold can be a hazard in mountain regions. The summer heatwave can become a killer when accompanied by high humidity.

Jetstreams are high-speed rivers of wind that blow around the temperate latitudes at about 6 miles (10km) up. Their speeds are around 100kt (c200km/hr) but can be stronger but often less strong. They are directly associated with the formation and movement of depressions and, in general, an intense depression accompanies a strong jet. When jets move from their normal regions then the depressions go too and weather in the area becomes unseasonal.

Latent heat is heat needed to make ice become water and water become water vapour. When the water vapour condenses back into water and the water becomes ice again, the latent heat is released. So the formation of clouds, rain and snow liberates vast amounts of heat at altitude. To get an idea of the quantity, heat up a litre of water in a pan with the lid on until it is on the point of boiling. Now take the lid off and heat it until it all boils away. The amount of heat energy you've used to turn that water into vapour is a bit more than would be given out by a small electric fire in half an hour. The sun evaporates vast quantities of water across the globe so the heat that is eventually delivered to the higher atmosphere is equally immense. When ice turns to water it gives only about one seventh of the heat required to turn the water into vapour.

Occlusions are the fronts most frequently experienced over land masses. They are formed late in the development of depressions when cold fronts overtake warm ones. This is a natural consequence of depression formation and it is another way in which the atmosphere raises warm air to altitude. This is because cold fronts undercut warm ones and lift the warm air aloft. Occlusions are often responsible for long periods of rain or snow which may be continuous or intermittent.

Precipitation is a generic word for all those meteorological events that fall from the sky such as rain, snow, drizzle and hail.

Tropopause is an invisible layer at around 40,000–50,000ft (12–15km) which limits the height of weather processes. When you see a majestic summer thundercloud that has a flat anvil-shaped top then you are seeing the tropopause. The tropopause is highest over the tropics and lowest over the Poles.

Troposphere is the shell of air below the tropopause where all the normal atmospheric processes take place. Above the troposphere is the stratosphere which does not influence every-day weather forecasting.

Types of cloud and useful conversions

Cloud types*
Note: Abbreviations such as St, Cu are the usual meteorological shorthand.
Low clouds include *stratus* (St) – fog-like cloud above the ground or shrouding hills and mountains; *cumulus* (Cu) – heap clouds of moderate extent; *stratocumulus* (Sc) heap clouds in layers. These clouds exist between ground and about 7000ft (0–2km)

Medium-level clouds include *altostratus* (As) – layer clouds often covering the whole sky and associated with bad weather; *altocumulus* (Ac) – rafts and islands of small heap clouds sometimes associated with thunder. These clouds exist between 7000 and 25,000ft (2–8km)

High level clouds include *cirrus* (Ci) – high, white, often feathery ice-crystal clouds; *cirrostratus* (Cs) – a milky veil of high white cloud giving haloes. These clouds exist between 16,000 and 45,000ft (5–13km)

6

* Not all common cloud types are covered here. For more information and the associated weather see Instant Weather Forecasting.

Abbreviations for climatic regions etc
NH = northern hemisphere; SH = southern hemisphere; TL = temperate latitudes; TC = tropical latitudes.

CONVERSIONS

Temperature conversion °C/°F

Temperatures above freezing

°C	45	40	35	30	25	20	15	10	5	0
°F	113	104	95	86	77	68	59	50	45	32

Temperatures below freezing

°C	-5	-10	-15	-20	-25	-30	-35	-40	-45	-50
°F	23	14	5	-4	-13	-22	-31	-40	-49	-58

Speed conversions
1 metre per second (m/s) = 2kt
1 kilometre per hour (km/hr) = 0.63 miles per hour (mi/hr)
1mi/hr = 1.6km/hr
1kt = 1.15mi/hr = 1.69m/s

Length and height conversions
1 mile = 1.6km
1 metre = 3.3ft   1ft = 0.3m
1000ft = 300m   10,000ft = 3km   40,000ft = 12km

Pressure conversions
1 millibar (mb) = 1 hectopascal (hPa)
1mb = 0.02953in of mercury   1000mb = 1 bar = 29.53in of mercury
Standard atmospheric pressure = 76cm of mercury = 1013mb

1 The world's winds and weather

The winds and major weather systems of the world tend to follow the patterns shown in Fig 1. Here are depicted the belts of predominantly high or low pressure that surround the Earth, but real weather patterns often diverge widely from this simple view. It really indicates what would happen if the Earth were covered entirely in water and no continents intervened. However, it is a good starting point for a study of the world's winds and the table on page 8 gives the major facts.

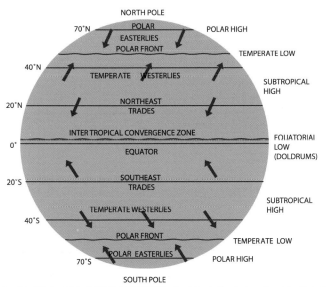

Other major wind systems

Semi-permanent lows

There are two major melting-pots for lows in the temperate latitudes of the northern hemisphere. One is in the North Atlantic near Iceland, the other occurs in the North Pacific near the Aleutian Islands. Here travelling lows formed along the Polar front (page 12) are absorbed. These are regions of almost permanent low pressure.

In the southern hemisphere the low-pressure melting-pots are close to Antarctica and so have little effect on the southern land masses.

The semi-permanent high pressure regions push ridges of high pressure into the temperate latitudes, especially in summer, and so bring good weather to climes which experience strings of lows during the winter. However, sometimes large anticyclones stick over temperate regions and prevent the lows from moving west to east. These are called *blocking highs*. A very strong anticyclone usually settles over Siberia in the depths of winter when temperatures are very low. Winds from the Siberian High produce much of the coldest weather of Europe and Asia.

In summer, travelling lows deepen over the land masses while highs become less intense. In winter, highs intensify over land and weaken over water.

Monsoons

These occur because pressure falls over hot landmasses in the summer when there is little comparable change over the surrounding seas. The Indian Ocean and China Sea monsoon comes from west or south-west. Northern India and surrounding regions become very hot in summer and a semi-permanent low forms. High pressure dominates the surrounding

Fig 1 The wind and pressure systems of a stylised world covered in water. Land masses will interfere with this simple image but generally the world's winds do conform to this scheme. The Inter-Tropical Convergence Zone (ITCZ) is shown in its northern hemisphere (NH) summer position. It will move to the other side of the Equator during the southern hemisphere (SH) summer.

Pressure belt	Rough latitudes	Main winds	Remarks
NORTHERN HEMISPHERE			
North Polar high	above 70°N	Polar easterlies	Winds over the pole are generally light. The polar easterlies blow out into the temperate low.
Temperate low	40 – 60°N	Temperate westerlies	Temperate westerlies meet the polar easterlies along a zone called the polar front where major storms are created, which travel west to east.
Subtropical high	20 – 40°N	Northeast trades	Warm westerlies blow out of this belt towards the polar front. Tropical revolving storms are born here.
Equatorial low	0 – 10°N	Light, variable	Often hot and sultry. Frequent heavy showers and thunderstorms along Inter-Tropical Convergence Zone (ITCZ).
SOUTHERN HEMISPHERE			
Equatorial low	0 – 10°S	Light variable	As above but ITCZ lies south of Equator in southern summer.
Subtropical high	20 – 40°S	Southeast trades	Most constant winds on Earth but they occasionally weaken or change direction.
Temperate low	40 – 60°S	Temperate westerlies	Tend to be NW (SW in NH). Zone of Roaring Forties.
Polar high	Below 70°S	Polar easterlies	Much windier than N Polar region. Can attain hurricane speeds.

seas. In India and the China Sea, the monsoon blows steadily from May to September accompanied by heavy rains and thunderstorms.

In winter, the pressure differences reverse and the monsoon blows from the north-east from October through to April and may reach gale force. The effect of the north Indian low is felt as far west as the eastern Mediterranean where it is responsible for the predominantly northerly winds in the Aegean and surrounding areas in summer.

There is a form of monsoon in north-western Australia in the dry season (April to November) with predominantly south-east winds. This gives way to the wet season (December to March) with north-west winds. The reversal comes about because the interior becomes extremely hot just as northern India does during the northern hemisphere summer. There is often intense and prolonged rainfall.

Sea breezes Minor monsoons occur in spring and summer when coastal land areas become hotter than their flanking seas. In Atlantic Europe, the breezes may not become stronger than 10–12kt but in Mediterranean-type latitudes they may reach as much as 20–25kt. Moist sea air which travels inland may be responsible for outbreaks of heavy thunderstorms.

Land breezes These occur coastwise overnight but they are mostly weak compared to sea breezes. However, if aided by katabatic winds from high ground inland, they can become a force to be reckoned with. They are then called falling or *fall* winds.

Mountains Many local fall winds are produced by mountains and sometimes, as in the case of the mistral of the northwest coasts of the Mediterranean, become significant over very large areas. The names and descriptions of some of these will be found on pages 60–61.

2 Bad weather systems

The world's weather is fuelled by heat from the sun and the water vapour produced by the evaporation of the sea and other bodies of water.

Wind, rain, snow etc occur when air flows of different temperatures come together. The major effect of the atmosphere is to lift warm air aloft by one means or another. It does this on a grand scale when a mass of warm, wet air meets a mass of colder wet air. The warm air masses breed over tropical and sub-tropical oceans and the large-scale surface winds waft them towards the Poles. Here they meet cold air masses that have gathered over Polar seas. The result is that millions of cubic kilometres of warm air are lifted in vast wedge-shaped layers over corresponding layers of cold air. When these two different air masses clash, it is almost as if they are fighting one another, so the dividing surfaces are called fronts. However, just like warring armies, they do not mix.

Most of our normal precipitation comes from fronts because when they occur depressions also start to form. So fronts and depressions are inextricably mixed. The depressions, together with their fronts, travel west to east because they are influenced by the upper westerly winds . As they travel, their central pressures fall – they *deepen* – and go through a life-cycle which includes becoming *occluded*; after occlusion the pressure rises until they cease to exist as organised entities. It is usually during the deepening phase that depressions produce the worst weather.

The other major means by which the atmosphere overturns is by convection. Warm air is wafted up while cool air comes down to take its place. Across the world – and especially in the tropics – immense heap clouds (cumulonimbus Cb) develop and, by means of updraughts, transport heated surface air to very high altitudes. At these altitudes they form snow which, as it falls, melts into rain that can be very intense and often accompanied by hail. The storms may become electrified and lightning and thunder result as part of the process.

Water vapour, lifted by one of these means, condenses into cloud and releases a vast amount of *latent heat*. When the water vapour further condenses into water droplets, more latent heat is released. This is the major way in which heat is transported from the Earth's surface to high altitude.

In general, the greater the difference in temperature between the air masses forming depressions, the more vigorous they are. However even depressions that are past their prime can become rejuvenated by drawing in fresh supplies of cold air. In this way, 'old' depressions can suddenly behave like young ones.

Wind speeds in severe wind storms are often very variable with differences of tens of knots in speed between places that may be only a few miles apart. Trees can be uprooted in one place, whereas trees in similar situations close by are unaffected. Severe gales occurring when the trees are in leaf can be devastating as happened in Spain, France and England during the great gale of October 1983 when many millions of trees were felled. In the extreme conditions that attended the Fastnet yacht race in August 1979, yachts caught by the storm in certain parts of the course were dismasted, sunk or abandoned with loss of life while yachts in other parts found the conditions manageable, although unusually bad. The same was experienced by participants in the Sydney to Hobart race of December 1998 where somewhat similar conditions were experienced and loss of life and craft also occurred.

Wind speeds associated with depressions are not as severe as those that accompany tropical revolving storms (TRS). There is little upper wind in the tropics to have an ameliorating affect on a TRS whereas they are part and parcel of depressions. The strongest winds in depressions rarely exceed 80kt (150km/hr) and then only in gusts, whereas in the TRS, wind speeds go to above 150kt (280km/hr). Even these winds are not as severe as those in tornadoes, where the scale of wind speeds goes as high as 280kt (480km/hr). Fortunately, such utterly devastating tornadoes are rare.

It is not wind speeds but wave conditions that produce disasters at sea; variability in the wind in both speed and direction in extreme conditions can produce waves that are unusual, both in their height and in the way they break. The typhoon that struck the United States Navy Task Force 38 off the Philippines in December 1944 sank three destroyers and drowned 790 men.

There are the occasional rogue waves that, due to a combination of circumstances, grow to over 80ft (24m) in height – some to as much as 100ft (30m) or more. In the North Atlantic in 1955 the RMS *Queen Elizabeth II* was struck by a 96ft (29m) high wave and almost laid over on her side. Any ship not fully battened down is liable to founder in these conditions and some do.

Depressions produce the storms of the temperate latitudes. Tropical revolving storms are, as the name indicates, storms of the tropics. They need the high surface temperatures of tropical seas to create and then maintain their immense energy. TRS do not cross the Equator but those of the northern hemisphere move westward on paths that normally take them to the right, to eventually re-curve and finally become demoted to depressions as they move eastwards.(see page 28) Those that occur on the other side of the Equator are called cyclones and affect Australasia, Indonesia, Oceania, Polynesia and the southern parts of the Indian Ocean. Those that occur in the northern part of the Indian Ocean are also called *cyclones* despite being in the northern hemisphere.

The monsoons of the Indian sub-continent and its surroundings occur on a yearly basis but sometimes fail. Then, instead of great floods, the areas suffer drought. Monsoons also occur in other tropical areas such as northern Australia and Indonesia.

Electric storms are more localised than depression storms and are infrequent in temperate latitudes. In the tropics they become the major

bad weather systems. It is the intense gusts that are generated around them and the lightning strikes that make them dangerous. They can also produce intense rainfall over limited areas and so lead to flash floods as well as damage to human and animal life and property when large hailstones fall. The most hazardous storms are the rapidly rotating tornadoes, the worst of which can completely obliterate small townships and lead to considerable loss of life.

Blizzards, ice storms and avalanches are also great hazards and need to be treated with respect. Their characteristics will be covered in the following pages.

Lows and highs

To understand a depression or low, it is helpful to know its life cycle. Families of lows form, grow to maturity and occlude along the Polar fronts of both hemispheres. We will use the situation in Fig 2 in the northern hemisphere to explain what happens. We have an occluding low (A) on the right; a low in the prime of life on the left (C) and between them an embryonic low (B) just forming. This continuous set of fronts are part of the Polar front which may well appear broken up on weather maps.

Both lows A and C started life like B – as a 'wave' in the Polar front. With time B may grow to look like C and then later still (some days) part of the cold front (blue spikes) will have overtaken the warm front (red lumps) to form an occluded front (A). This low lifecycle is directed and governed by the jetstream which blows some 6 miles (10km) up and the lows develop a few hundred miles on its Equatorial side. (By the time the low is occluded, the jet coincides with the point of occlusion).

Rain breaks out (green shading) ahead of the warm front, behind the cold front and around the top of the low. The jets move further away from the Equator in the summer and tend to ease back again during the winter. This is why Atlantic Europe experiences more frequent and stronger depressions during the winter than during the summer.

Waves like B tend to move fast (typically 40kt or 60km/hr) but slow down as they develop into lows like C. As the air sandwiched between the warm and cold fronts of C is warm and humid so C is called a warm-sector depression. *Warm-sector depressions* will usually have the stormiest weather because the central pressure of C will fall with time and so 'tighten' the isobars. As soon as the low starts to occlude, its central pressure will begin to rise and then the low is said to be *filling-up*.

With a travelling occlusion, the rain may be lighter and possibly intermittent. However, old systems like A can rejuvenate by absorbing a new draught of cold air from Polar regions. Further, a primary low can produce gales when another secondary one invades its circulation. Fig 2 also shows features of the weather map. Isobars join lines of equal pressure and the winds near the surface follow them like trams on tramlines. They blow to keep LOW pressure on their LEFT (in the northern hemisphere, RIGHT in the southern hemisphere). Salients sticking out from lows towards surrounding highs are *troughs*. Weather deteriorates in troughs with possible very heavy showers.

Anticyclones or highs usually produce better weather and lighter winds with the isobars much more widely spaced. Ridges of high pressure bringing more benign weather occupy the spaces between the members of a family of travelling depressions. However, travelling highs often invade the regions where lows are endemic. The weather in the centre of highs tends to be fair with light winds but this may vary on their periphery. A situation in which very strong winds can occur is when a travelling low comes up against a more-or-less stationary high. If the high does not yield, very strong winds will blow between the two.

Sometimes when the weather remains good for days or weeks, the reason is that a great *blocking high* has interposed itself in the normal run of lows and ridges around the hemisphere. Lows are then diverted

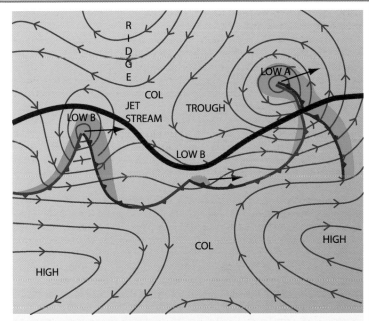

Fig 2 Features of a weather map.

to areas north and south of their normal tracks. For example, sometimes when the summer weather is fair over western Europe then it is poorer than usual in the Mediterranean region. Blocking highs bring some of the best summer weather although they can be responsible for heatwaves. In winter they may bring days or weeks of overcast conditions as well as very light winds in which smogs (smoke fogs) form. These days the smoke is more likely to be exhaust fumes from vehicles. Los Angeles is well-known for its smogs and in Britain the great London smog of December 1952 was responsible for at least 12,000 deaths. This tragedy led to the Clean Air Acts and there has not been a similar occurrence in the UK since.

The region between two highs and two lows is called a *col*. Weather in cols is indeterminate but the wind will be light and variable. Salients sticking out from centres of high pressure towards lows are *ridges*. For example, there is a pronounced ridge ahead of low C (Fig 2) where the weather will be fair but it will change to a *frontal trough* when the warm front arrives.

While Polar-front depressions are the most common, there are other kinds of lows that bring bad weather. *Polar lows* come down from Polar sea areas and are very cold and wet (or snowy). Thundery lows develop in hot periods and produce some of the worst thunderstorms. Small lows can invade most regions at any time and produce more localised wind and rain (or snow) which is possibly dangerous as they can move rapidly and produce unexpected gales. Some regions are notorious for spawning new depressions notably the Gulf of Genoa in the Mediterranean and Alberta in Canada.

Photo 1 During severe gales, the sea produces so much spray that visibility is impaired and salt is carried far inland.

3 Gales and tidal surges

Wind force

Strong winds cause damage because the pressure exerted by the wind increases as the square of the wind speed. This means that if the wind speed doubles, its effect on trees, buildings and sailing boats at sea increases by four times. For instance, Beaufort force 4 is around a mean speed of 13kt and this is about the best speed for recreational yachting. However, by doubling that speed, the pressure exerted becomes four times greater. It is not surprising therefore that storm force winds of around 50kt are extremely dangerous for yachts and the Beaufort description says that, while very rare on land, trees will be uprooted and there will be considerable structural damage.

The Beaufort Scale of wind force (*right*) covers some 12 categories but here we need only review the stronger ones – those of force 6 *strong breeze* or above. These are sustained wind speeds but gusts can be as much as twice the mean speeds. For speeds experienced in hurricanes, typhoons etc. see page 30.

Gale-force winds

Depressions, whose central pressure falls rapidly with time, will generate gale-force or severe gale-force winds. The strongest winds usually appear maybe 100 miles or more away from the low centre and on the Equatorial side. Winds are often much lighter on the Polar side of depressions.

If you have a barometer the actual height of the instrument is not important. It is the rate at which the barometer falls or rises that matters; this is known as the tendency. Normally tendencies are less than one or two millibars per three-hour period (the period over which meteorologists measure tendency). However, it is more practical for us to measure a barometer's change over an hour. There is often a relationship between

BEAUFORT SCALE				
Force	Speed (kt)	Land description	Sea state	
6 Strong breeze	22 – 27	Large branches in motion. Whistling in wires.	Large waves form. Extensive foam crests. Much spray off waves	
7 Near gale*	28 – 33	Whole trees in motion. Resistance felt when walking against wind.	Sea heaps up and white streaks blown along wind direction.	
8 Gale**	34 – 40	Twigs broken off trees. Walking impeded. Rare inland.	Moderately high waves of greater length. Crests break into spindrift. Foam in well-marked streaks.	
9 Strong gale	41 – 47	Chimney pots and slates removed. Fences blown down.	High waves. Crests begin to topple and roll over.	
10 Storm ***	48 – 55	Very rare inland. Trees uprooted. Considerable structural damage.	Very high waves with long overhanging crests. Whole sea surface appears white Visibility impaired.	
11 Violent storm	56 – 63	An exceptional event.	Exceptionally high waves. Sea completely covered in long patches of white foam. Visibility impaired.	
12 Hurricane	64 +	A once-in-a-lifetime event. Sea spray blown great distances inland. Forests levelled.	Immense waves arch over and capsize small craft. Structural damage to ships.	

(In American usage * *Moderate gale* ** *Fresh gale* *** *Whole gale*)

the tendency and the wind that accompanies or follows it. You must realise that this is only a rule-of-thumb interpretation but we can say that when gales are gathering then a tendency of:

> 1 millibar* per hour will lead to winds of force 6
> 2 millibars per hour will lead to force 8
> 3 millibars per hour will lead to force 9–10
>
> * In some countries the hectoPascal (hPa) replaces the mb but they are exactly the same unit.

It is only near the centres of rapidly deepening and very active depressions that tendencies of 2–3mb/hour are normally experienced. However, the rises (often very sharp) that occur immediately after the lowest pressure is reached can be accompanied by even stronger winds. *First rise after low foretells a stronger blow.*

The most prevalent direction for gale to storm-force winds is south to south-west (NH) or north to north-west (SH). Once the trough has passed, the new wind direction is most likely to be west to north-west (NH) or south-west to west (SH). An indicator of the potentially catastrophic shift is an 'eye of the storm' lightening of the winds.

Isobars and *fronts* are the main constituents of weather maps (Fig 3). Where isobars are close together the wind is strongest while fronts may be the venue for sudden squalls and changes of wind direction.

Depressions, with a few exceptions, travel west to east in both hemispheres and often the flanking high-pressure systems are relatively static. The difference in pressure with distance is called the *gradient of the isobars*. A steep gradient indicates strong wind and if a travelling depression 'collides' with a more static high, the gradient between them steepens and may lead to gale or severe gale-force winds. Similar things happen when a primary low slows and a secondary low invades its circulation. Winds can become very strong in some areas while in others

Fig 3a A stylised depression in the northern hemisphere. Winds blow anticlockwise around low centres and clockwise round highs. The depression as a whole moves west to east. At positions where the isobars are close together, winds are likely to be gale-force or more.

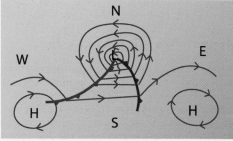

Fig 3a

Fig 3b The similar situation is shown in the southern hemisphere. Now winds blow clockwise about lows and anticlockwise about highs. In both cases, the sector of warm air between the warm front (red) and the cold front (blue) face their respective subtropical highs. Depressions in both hemispheres move west to east. Again positions with close isobars will be where the strongest winds will be found.

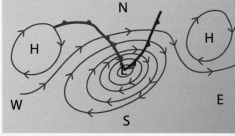

Fig 3b

they lighten. The strongest winds will usually be found on the equatorial side of the low while on the Polar side winds may be very light.

Storm surges and seiches

Strong wind has a considerable frictional drag on water. The storm surge that produced the catastrophic coastal flooding in Britain and the Low Countries in 1953 was induced by the constant strong-to-gale force northerly wind that blew between a high to the west of Scotland and a low over Scandinavia. This entrained the water into and down the North Sea and so prevented the tide from flowing out at one stage. The next tide grew on its back leading to exceptional tidal height. The waves battering the sea defences did the rest. A contributory factor lay in the way the North Sea grows narrower as you come south. Similar topography is found in the English Channel when the wind is south-west or west. Thus tidal surges occasionally occur in the central and eastern channel. In the Mediterranean, southerly scirroco gales sometimes blow out of North Africa and raise the sea levels at Genoa, for example, by as much as 10ft (3m).

Large bodies of inland water such as the Great Lakes experience significant seiches (pronounced *sayshes*); when the wind blows steadily at gale force, the water level on the leeward side is raised by several feet thereby flooding low-lying coastal areas. It is correspondingly lowered on the windward side. When the wind eases the water levels oscillate like a see-saw until they come to rest.

The greatest surges of all are caused by underwater tectonic movements or earthquakes and are called *tsunamis*. The resulting wave energy travels at high speed across any intervening water. Ships at sea do not notice any significant change in height but once the tsunami comes into coastal waters it first draws the water back out to sea and follows it with a catastrophic tidal surge that may heap up to 100ft (30m) or more as it sweeps away the coastal infrastructure. The Indian Ocean tsunami of 26 December 2004 was the second largest earthquake to be recorded on a seismograph and 230,000 deaths are attributed to it. One positive result is that much better early warning systems are being developed.

Tips for recognising bad weather approaching will be covered on pages 16-18.

Photo 2 Force 8 inland can be highly damaging to trees in leaf.

4 Wind storms

In temperate latitudes, most of the wind storms come when the centres of deep depressions track across the country to the north of us (NH) or to the south (SH).

We saw earlier that the way in which depressions form leads to fronts developing, producing rain, drizzle, snow etc. Fronts produce precipitation in bands that often lasts for many hours. Warm fronts spread cloud and rain hundreds of miles ahead of where they meet the surface while cold fronts have their cloud and rain behind them, and are not so extensive. The rain from warm fronts is fairly continuous whereas that from cold fronts is continuous at first with heavy, often squally, showers. It then reverts to continuous but lighter rain; after a period of high cloud, it breaks to blue sky. Showers usually follow. Occluded fronts, have the precipitation pattern of a warm front that changes, normally without a break, into that of a cold front.

Lows are like heat engines – they generate most power when the difference in temperature between their hottest and coldest parts is greatest. So winter sees the most powerful depressions with wind speeds typically growing to 50 to 60kt in some parts.

There are regions where pressure is almost permanently low and one of these is to be found south of Iceland. Other lows that invade the space south of the Icelandic low pressure region can bring very strong winds to the seas off the coasts of Atlantic Europe; sometimes such wild weather is not confined to the winter half of the year.

Recognising coming trouble

Strong surface weather is allied to virile jetstreams (See page 10). If the main axis of the jets moves north (NH), as it usually does in a NH summer, then cyclonic weather moves north as well. The jets move further south (north in SH) in winter bringing their depressions with them. If, as sometimes happens, the jets are reluctant to move with the seasons, places that should have good summers will experience more of an autumn or winter regime with much rain and cool conditions.

Jetstreams cannot be seen but you can see the characteristic clouds that accompany them (photo 3, page 17). Jet cirrus is very high ice-cloud that forms just on the Equatorial side of the jet in both hemispheres. Its trademarks are lines or banners which converge towards the horizon. Despite their height, if the individual elements of cirrus cloud can easily be seen scudding across the sky then the winds up there may be as strong as 120kt or more. That means a strong jet and strong wind usually follows at the surface some time (maybe as much as 12 or even 24 hours) later. So looking at cirrus can help you to foretell the severity of coming weather (see photos 3 and 4). However, not all cirrus cloud foretells bad weather because it forms under many circumstances.

The weather forecasters have become very adept at recognising when storms are likely. However, they cannot say exactly *when* any weather element will reach you. For that you need to study the way the clouds and wind are developing. Guidance on this is given in my books *Instant Weather Forecasting*, *The Weather Handbook* and *Weather Wise*. However, as a rough guide, the arrival of cirrus cloud will usually only result in wind and rain when it is followed by a characteristic sequence of clouds and wind shifts, (page 18).

Photo 3 Here is a sky some hours before a severe gale blew up. It has important characteristics. Firstly the cloud is cirrus (Ci) – very high ice-crystal cloud that shows no shadows. The individual cloud elements form long banners. These show the wind direction at something like six miles up. Despite their height, the parallel line effect shows that the clouds are moving. This indicates they are being carried by a strong jetstream which is linked to strong surface weather. This is a sky foretelling gales – possibly severe gales – later.

Preparing for a gale

Keep an eye on the forecasts and monitor the sky and the way the wind is shifting direction. If you have a barometer, check to see if it is falling fairly steadily. You may not know how bad it will get but you can take some precautions. Will all the doors and windows of your house close securely? Are you worried about the state of chimneystacks? If so, keep away from rooms where they might fall in. It is unusual for there to be a lot of rain when winds are high but in winter, piled snow may prevent you opening windward doors. If you think snow is likely, keep a shovel in the house.

Outside the house, lay ladders, garden furniture and other such items down on the ground. If you have a portable gazebo, consider whether you should take it down. Will the rubbish bins be blown over? Should you move the car, the boat or caravan away from the reach of trees that might be blown down? Are there any items outside which may become missiles in a high wind? Could fences be blown down on anything valuable that can be moved? If you must go outside at the height of the storm, try to do so on the leeward side of the house.

If driving and the conditions become very bad, stop somewhere clear of trees. Take great care when overtaking high-sided vehicles. Avoid, if possible, elevated roads and bridges. Ferries may be cancelled in storm conditions. However, if you do travel by sea, have you got seasickness tablets? If you live on the coast, could this wind, together with a high tide, produce coastal flooding where you are? Coastal campers and caravanners should think seriously of moving inland well before the worst of the wind hits. This is particularly important if your campsite is up on the cliffs.

STORM INDICATORS	
Cloud formations	**Comment**
Cirrus Ci	Long lines or banners (photo 3). Individual Ci elements may appear like little hooks. Ci usually travel swiftly from the west. Surface wind may not increase much at first. After period of hours then look for:
Cirrostratus Cs	Sun or moon surrounded by a ring halo (photo 4). Wind should have shifted during preceding hours from a westerly to a southerly point and increased (SH northerly point)
Altostratus As	Sun or moon disappears into darker mass of layer cloud. This precedes rain (or snow). Wind should have strengthened
Nimbostratus Ns	Cloudbase lowers and rain (or snow) commences. If preceding a storm, wind will now be strong, maybe gale force.

After the sequence of events outlined above, the rain will probably cease but very cloudy conditions will normally prevail for a time. As time passes there will be a continuation of rain or drizzle as fronts pass; this is usually accompanied by wind shifts and sometimes squalls. Gale-force winds are often quite variable in speed with some periods of wind-increase to storm force or more followed by lesser strength. At sea, visibility will be greatly deteriorated by spray, drizzle etc., especially following warm fronts. Force 8 gales are very rare inland but gusts may increase wind strength locally to force 12 or more. Whether at sea or inland, gust speeds are going to be much the same, so gale damage to trees and property is usually due to gusts.

If wind speed decreases markedly and other factors do not change much, you may be experiencing an *eye of the storm* event as a low centre passes over you, only for the wind to pick up strongly again from another direction.

Photo 4 Ring haloes round the sun (or moon) form a milky veil of cirrostratus cloud. These haloes often foretell approaching rain or snow and very probably gales too.

5 Thunderstorms

As shown by the cell theory (see pages 21 and 22), thunderstorms can be **single cell** or **multiple cell**. In addition there may be upper level storms and a much more intense form called a **supercell**. Single-cell storms give short periods of thunder and lightning with big gaps between. They occur, for example, along cold fronts and in fleets of shower clouds.

Multiple-cell storms are what most people know as thunderstorms and they may last for hours. Upper level storms form perhaps 8000–10,000ft (2.5–3km) up over the surfaces of fronts. Supercells are immense single-cell storms which may spawn tornadoes and giant hailstones.

Thunder rolls are caused by reflections of sound from surrounding thunderheads as well as from multiple lightning flashes. To find how far away you are from the lightning, count the seconds between flash and thunder and divide by three for distance in kilometres and by five for distance in miles. Do not expect to hear thunder if the storm is more than 10 miles (16km) away although it can, when the conditions are right, be heard as much as 16 miles (20km) away. In addition, you can detect thundery activity through *sky-ray transmission* of thunder. This will sound like big guns being fired and may come from storms as much as 100 miles or more (150+ km) away because the sound is deflected from high-level layers of the atmosphere.

Type of storm	When	Where	Frequency and type of lightning	Previous weather	Duration of storm in one place	Risk of tornadoes	Comments
Single cell	Any time of year. Most prevalent spring and autumn	Showery airstreams and along cold fronts	Low, forked	Big shower heads. Can be quite windy. Sudden gusts and hail when fronts pass in winter	Often passes quickly – a clap and it's gone!	Very occasionally Class 1 or 2 (see page 34)	Unstable, showery airstreams behind depressions. Hail small if at all
Multiple cell	Mainly summer and autumn (TL). Any time (TC)	Hot humid areas inland	Generally a few per minute. Forked	Humid, light winds. Big Cb clouds. Fitful gusts. Some storms come up against the wind	Maybe an hour or more – can last for hours	Sometimes up to Class 3 but not often in TC	Typically the storm of summer afternoons in TC. Small hail may lay deep. Local flooding
Upper level	As above	Around hot landmasses	Sometimes very frequent – mainly sheet but some forked	Gathering thundery-looking cloud. Warm to hot, close. Light to moderate winds, gusty	Duration often measured in hours	Very unlikely	Hail is unusual but can produce a downpour
Supercells	In areas prone to this type of storm, from spring into autumn	TL occasionally. More prevalent in areas such as Southern USA	Very frequent and intense. Forked and sheet	Gathering black or even coloured cloud. Very oppressive. Wind towards storm	Together with build-up may last hours	Supercells spawn tornadoes so always consider risk	Often giant hail damages cars, boats, caravans etc. Can be lethal to humans and animals so seek adequate shelter. High risk of flooding. Big gusts

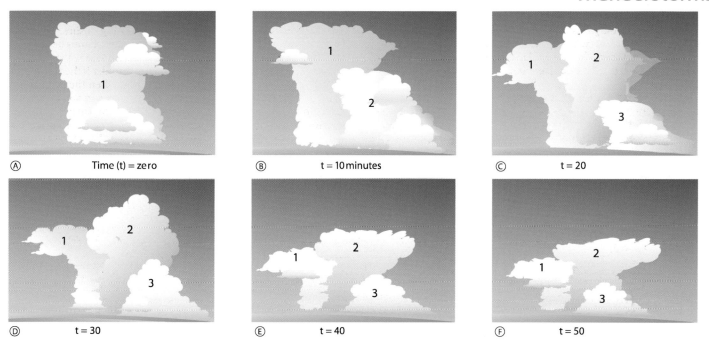

Fig 4 An individual storm cell will only produce thunder and lightning for less than half an hour. Yet thunderstorms may go on for hours. This can be explained by an actual example of a family of storms. These are interpretations of actual photos of a set of cells developing during a period of about an hour. The wind is blowing the cells away from us. At (A) a large thunder cloud (1) develops. It has a knobbly top and so is at its most active, generating lightning, heavy rain and hail. Ten minutes later (B), a daughter cell (2) has developed beside the ageing (1) which is developing an anvil top. Ten minutes (C) after this stage the daughter has itself developed a daughter (3). At (D) ten minutes after this, (2) has gone through its most active phase while (3) has not developed much. At (E), cell (2) is developing its anvil top while (3) is not going to grow into a full storm because it is too late in the afternoon. In the end (F) we have two aged storms and the second generation daughter (3) and the storm is over. So as one cell grows too old it generates another to take over – just like life.

Thunderstorms

It is difficult to gauge the severity of storms and this may not be mentioned in forecasts. Tropical thunderstorms will usually be more intense than experienced in temperate latitudes (TL). In Mediterranean-type latitudes they can be quite frequent, occurring on as many as half the summer days and autumn months in some places. Parts of the western and central Mediterranean can get up to 10 inches of rain in one day in the autumn months due to thundery outbreaks. In the south of the USA big storms occur at most times of the year with consequent risk of tornadoes.

Intense storms are more likely on higher ground and can spawn flash floods when the precipitated water pours down the valleys. Thus storms inland should not be ignored as the water will take time to get to you (see page 48).

Storms can be induced in the afternoons over coastal hinterlands due to seabreezes bringing in cooler, very humid air over already-heated land.

Is it coming my way?

When you first hear thunder you cannot rely on the wind direction you can feel to tell you which way the storm is moving. Before the storm clouds fully arrive, try to monitor the direction that the medium-level clouds (altocumulus/altostratus) are moving. This is most likely to be the direction the storm, as a whole, is moving. Storms can create their own surface winds because the heavy rain and hail drag down air, which then spreads around the storm cells like pouring cream onto a plate. At the leading edges, the downdraught wind and the ordinary wind combine to produce often very strong gusts while in the rear the two work against one another, creating a calmer sector. When several storm cells follow one another, there will often be a roller-coaster of savage winds, thunder, lightning, heavy rain and hail interspersed with quieter periods.

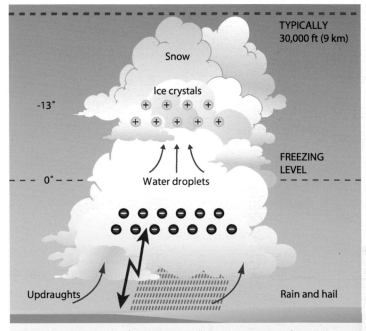

Fig 5 The anatomy of a thunderstorm cell in its most active phase. A negative charge congregates in the lower reaches of the cloud and induces a positive charge in the earth. The result is lightning.

Photo 5 A great thunder cloud catches the setting sun. It throws into relief its anvil-shaped top and the solidity of the cloud mass beneath. There seems to be much more cloud behind so it could indicate a major weather shift

You cannot have a thunderstorm without lightning because thunder is simply the sound waves energised by the expansion of the air along the path of a lightning flash. To create lightning, storm clouds need to reach into the levels of the atmosphere with temperatures below −13°C, where ice crystals can form (Fig 5). In the rarefied atmosphere of clouds, water droplets do not freeze until they are well below the normal freezing point of 0°C. Strong updraughts in thunder clouds, either vertical or angled, lift water droplets to high levels at speeds that may be as high as 60mph (30m/s) resulting in the separation of vast quantities of positive and negative electric charge.

Mechanisms within the cloud, which are not fully understood even today, mean that charged particles bring concentrations of negative charge into the bases of storm clouds while positive accumulations exist at higher levels. The negative bases induce positive charge in the earth below and when the electric stress becomes too great, the potential difference is lowered by the giant sparks we call lightning springing between them. As the ice crystals/water vapour regime seems to be necessary for the separation of the electric charge in the cloud – and as this is the same combination that results in heavy rain – so deluges of rain and/or hail accompany electric storms.

Point action and electric winds

If you have an electrically-charged pointed metal object it will lose charge very rapidly. Lightning conductors are attached to such pointed objects and connected by thick copper strips to the earth, acquiring the same positive potential as the earth under a thunder cloud. This causes an *electric wind* of positive ions to stream upwards from the point into the cloud above. This is called *point action*. There, the positive charges combine with the negative charges and so lower the potential. This may well deter a strike. If a strike does occur then the conductor provides a path to guide it to earth.

Precautions

The best place to avoid a lightning strike is indoors or in a car. If you are out in the open you are a very likely target, especially if you put up an umbrella or are carrying items like golf clubs. If you cannot reach adequate shelter then adopt the stance recommended under Lightning in the mountains given below. Do not believe that because the storm is not yet overhead that you are safe. Lightning has been known to strike miles from the storm from which it originated. Strikes can occur literally *out of the blue*. Such *dry* strikes seem to carry a greater punch than those occurring where it is raining.

Sheltering under broad-leaf trees such as oaks can be dangerous but grouped conifers are rarely struck. This is thought to be because of the *point action* of their needles.

At home, isolate the outside TV aerial by disconnecting it. Your TV and computer may have modems that are connected to the telephone cables. So remove the telephone plug if you have not fitted a surge suppressor. Your house does not have to be physically struck to sustain damage; local strikes may generate earth currents that can enter your electrical system. Surge suppressors should be included in the circuits of vulnerable equipment such as TVs and computers.

As far as possible ensure that animals are safe. Herds of sheep and cows are prone to strikes that can kill and maim as they jump from animal to animal. Get horses into stables, and dogs and cats indoors.

If you own a yacht you should have a lightning conductor fitted that stands proud above aerials or any other protuberances at the top of the mast. This is particularly important for yachts with masts stepped on the deck. To improve safety, try to avoid standing near to rigging or heavy metal deck gear such as winches.

Photo 6 A thunderstorm over Mclean's Ridge, New South Wales, Australia. The forked lightning is accompanied by sheet lightning from discharges within the mass of cloud. PHOTO: MICHAEL BATH

Types of lightning

Forked lightning is almost instantaneous. Prior to a strike, an invisible leader stroke, travelling at some 100 miles per second (160km/second) builds in steps (there may be 40 or more of them) from the cloud to the ground. Then, within a relatively short distance of the ground, the stroke we actually see (the return stroke) leaps back up the path to discharge the cloud above. When the cloud base is high, cloud to cloud lightning may travel for great distances more-or-less horizontally below the cloudbase.

Sheet lightning is simply the reflection of lightning occurring between the cloud elements (see photo 6). As the lightning does not come to ground, this form has always been recognised as non-dangerous. However, strong ground strikes can also occur in storms where sheet lightning mainly occurs, as the photo also proves.

Sheet lightning usually occurs with high-level storms and can be seen for many miles further than the thunder can penetrate. The resulting displays are often fascinating to watch. However, when you hear thunder take appropriate action.

In tropical storms, multiple strokes (perhaps five or more) are more likely. Also in the tropics, storms erupt very frequently with an average of up to 80 days a year compared to 20 at the most in southeast England; this is the part of Britain where storms are most frequent.

Ball lightning: after a powerful stroke of lightning (usually at the end of a storm) a glowing ball is sometimes formed not far above the ground. This ball, which may vary between an inch and several feet in diameter, is usually bluish white and appears to be attracted to rooms. It has been known to come down chimneys and so enter a living room. It will explode on meeting a metal object that is earthed, such as a kitchen range. In the open air it usually bowls along at a slow speed and can therefore be avoided. Even if you are close, resist any temptation to touch one.

Lightning in the mountains

Storms in mountainous or hilly districts are more frequent than on lowlands and are, like most storms, more likely in the afternoon. They need warm or hot, quiet weather in the mornings to develop. In latitudes like those of the Mediterranean they can be very frequent and quite violent, especially in the eastern Mediterranean and the Balkan lands to the north.

Lightning is the greatest hazard in the mountains. Immediate signs of the electrical charging of the atmosphere will possibly include a tingling of your scalp and your body experiencing a creepy feeling. You may see St Elmo's fire – a blue light flickering round the tops of rods or poles – indicating that a lightning strike may be imminent.

When a strike occurs, ground currents are generated and strikes are most likely on pinnacles, rock outcrops and cairns higher up. So although they seem the most inviting refuges, it is dangerous to shelter below or under rock faces or in the small declivities near the base of a cliff as the ground currents from strikes above will tend to travel through you. Despite probable exposure to wind and rain sit (hugging drawn-up legs) out on fairly level ground some way from the elbow where rock face meets flatter ground. Avoid anything that is isolated and pointed skywards. If you are using ropes, make sure you are not connected to one hanging down the rock face.

Photo 7 When frontal storms are approaching the clouds often take on strange forms. Here a buzzard soars in the unstable air that is responsible for the lines of altostratus cloud. You may not hear thunder yet, but it cannot be long delayed.

7 Tropical revolving storms

In the tropics (between about 24°N and 24°S) the warmth of the seas leads to the spawning of large tropical revolving storms (TRS). These have different names depending on where they occur.

Storms very similar to TRS also occur in the Mediterranean, although only every 10 to 20 years.

Hurricanes

These usually start very weakly near the Cape Verde islands off the coast of Africa as *tropical depressions*. When they intensify, they become *tropical storms*, which typically occurs within two days. As they develop and when the winds exceed 74 mph (120 km/h) they are classed as *hurricanes*. They move west to northwest and gather strength from the heat of the sea surface as well as from the release of heat when their clouds and rain form. They have a clear centre – the eye – (see photo 8) in which the winds are deceptively light, surrounded by circulating winds that grow in velocity to produce gusts exceeding 100kt (180km/h).

The intensity of hurricane winds is given by the Saffir-Simpson scale which strictly only applies to hurricanes in the North Atlantic and the North Pacific east of the International Date Line. However, the scales used elsewhere are very similar.

Storm surges The stress of the winds on the sea leads to a heightening of the coastal waters. Surges that occur with the categories of hurricanes are as follows.

Cat 1 = 4–5ft (1.2–1.5m);	Cat 2 = 6–8ft (1.8–2.4m);
Cat 3 = 9–12ft (2.7–3.7m);	Cat 4 = 13–18ft (4–5.5m);
Cat 5 = above 18ft (5.5m)	

Name	Location	Season	Remarks
Hurricanes	North Atlantic tropical seas. Central America. Caribbean, Gulf of Mexico, Southern USA	May to October	Very damaging because of population densities in the areas they ravage. Winds up to 200kt. Lifespan of days and weeks
Typhoons	Northwest Pacific	May to November. Even some in winter months	There are more typhoons than hurricanes in a season
Cyclones	Indian Ocean including Persian Gulf, East Africa, Malaysia, Northern Australia Micronesia and Polynesia	December to April	Extensive loss of life in low-lying area such as Bangladesh
Willy-willies	North Australia, Philippines etc.	December to April	Local name for cyclones

Photo 8 Hurricane Andrew over the Gulf of Mexico at 8.20 p.m. (GMT) on 25 August,1992, one of the most destructive hurricanes in US history. Note the eye and the cloud tops swirling round it. No ordinary depression would look so symmetrical. PHOTO COURTESY OF NASA

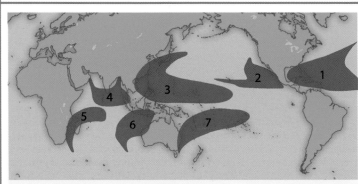

Fig 6 TRS areas of the world. **1** Atlantic basin – hurricanes; **2** North-east Pacific basin – hurricanes; **3** North-west Pacific basin – typhoons; **4** North Indian basin – cyclones; **5** South-west Indian basin – cyclones; **6** South-east Indian/Australian basin – cyclones; **7** South-west Pacific basin – cyclones

HURRICANE STRENGTHS		
Category	Strongest gusts	Effects
1	Below 77mph (120km/h)	Damage to some crops, trees, caravans
2	77–106mph (120–170km/h)	Heavy crop and minor structural damage. Small craft break moorings
3	106–140mph (170–220km/h)	Roof and structural damage. Likely power failure
4	140–175mph (220–280km/h)	Dangerous flying debris. Widespread power failure
5	Above 175mph (280km/h)	Widespread damage. Extensive coastal flooding

For those visiting or living in coastal areas that are hurricane prone, the storm surge may be the most disturbing hurricane phenomenon, which generally entails evacuation to inland areas. In 1899 the Bathurst Bay hurricane in Australia (Cyclone Mahina) produced a storm surge of such magnitude that dolphins and fish were found on the tops of 50ft (15m) cliffs.

Tropical storms have winds between 39 and 73mph (63–117km/h) and surges of 3ft or below while the winds of tropical depressions are below 38mph (below 62km/h) and have very small surges.

Most hurricanes affect the Caribbean and surrounding lands and islands but some cross the Yucatan Peninsula and threaten the west coast of central America bringing hurricane conditions to resorts like Acapulco. The majority of the extensive damage is due to the wind but in coastal areas it is the surges that are the most dangerous and contribute most to loss of life. Hurricanes, when they leave the sea, rapidly lose their strength but still constitute a hazard to inland areas. Hurricane Katrina (2005) which breached the levees at New Orleans produced damage that amounted to $81 billion in total losses.

As they approach the Gulf of Mexico and land areas of the eastern United States, hurricanes' paths tend to re-curve so that not all come ashore. As they re-cross the North Atlantic and move towards the coasts of Atlantic Europe they become less strong and are demoted to depressions but in autumn they can still produce strong to gale-force winds and carry echoes of tropical conditions into the areas they affect.

Typhoons

Typhoons are TRS that occur in the Northwest Pacific Basin and can be more intense than hurricanes. They effect China, Japan and surrounding lands and islands of the region. The origins of typhoons come from clusters of thunderstorms over sea temperatures of 80°F

(27°C) or more. Interacting tradewinds initiate rotation while rising air lowers pressure aloft and the typhoon intensifies. The tropical depression develops into a typhoon in a matter of hours, or it can take a few days.

Cyclones

These are the hurricanes of the Western Pacific. They affect Papua New Guinea, Micronesia and Polynesia and can travel as far south as New Zealand. When the El Niño phenomenon is neutral in the western areas, cyclones are more likely, while they are less likely in the island groups further east.

The town of Darwin, Australia was devastated by Cyclone Tracy on Christmas morning 1974; 65 people were killed and 70 per cent of homes were either destroyed or damaged.

Preparations for tropical storms

During the local season for tropical storms, make sure that you keep in touch with the media, who will broadcast advice. You will need to make some preparations in advance. In extreme cases, evacuation of coastal areas will be mandatory. In such an event, have you got essential items ready?

Evacuation Unless you have several days' notice of the storm coming, you are very unlikely to be able to fly out of the area at short notice. It might be best to load up your car and head inland to pre-arranged accommodation when it seems likely that a TRS is heading towards you. Have you got a good map of the area? Has your temporary accommodation got adequate shutters on the windows? Is it a solidly-built structure? Trailers are death-traps in winds of hurricane strength.

If you have a pet it must be evacuated with you (unless you can board it somewhere safe) plus of course several days' supply of food and water. If you seek shelter in evacuation centres or shelters in the US remember that no pets are allowed.

Essential supplies Remember that when danger threatens, people start panic-buying and essential supplies soon run out at the shops. Bottled water for drinking is a must, but you should also have plastic containers of water for washing. You need to make a list of essential items such as a camping stove, waterproof matches or a lighter, a kettle and saucepans (and means of cleaning them). Canned foods, chocolate and cereal bars will keep you going even when finding fresh food is proving difficult. As there are likely to be power failures, you will need flashlights and lanterns, a battery powered radio and back-up batteries. Also add a first-aid kit, bedding, waterproofs, durable clothing and plenty of toilet paper and paper towels. A roll of refuse bags can be very handy. Draw cash out so you are not reliant on ATM machines.

Children will need to be kept occupied wherever you are as it may be too hazardous to go out. Take a digital camera, board and card games, puzzle books, drawing paper and pens, crayons and favourite toys.

Insurance If you own a property in a storm-prone area then check your insurance – for instance in the US it is not standard policy to insure against flood damage and you will need a separate policy in advance. If you are renting you may be able to take out a renter's insurance. If you happen to be on vacation or on a business trip, think about what your situation would be if the hotel or apartment is badly damaged or flooded. Do you have a contingency plan?

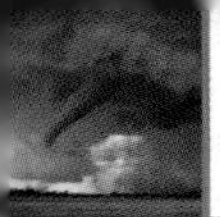

8 Tornadoes and waterspouts

Tornadoes are violent wind storms, often very localised, that can occur almost anywhere given the right circumstances. There are regions, however, where they are more frequent than elsewhere. The most tornado-prone area is *Tornado alley*, an area of the southern states of the USA where tornadoes are endemic. Waterspouts are usually lesser tornadoes that occur over bodies of water.

How tornadoes form

Tornadoes occur in association with cumulonimbus clouds where there are strong updraughts. Thunder may also occur. Converging winds near the ground are also an important factor in the formation of strong tornadoes. The more severe tornadoes breed in *supercells* (see page 20). Lesser tornadoes are often associated with sharp cold fronts where sudden changes in wind direction occur. (See table on page 34)

Weak is the general description for T0–T3 (F0–F1) and it is unusual to experience anything stronger in Europe and temperate latitudes. While Britain has a very large number of tornadoes, they are weak and only occasionally strengthen to T4 (F3). The Birmingham tornado of Thursday 28 July 2005 caused millions of pounds in damage and was one of the strongest recent tornadoes in England but it was still only on the edge of being a T4.

Tornadoes are not confined to the summer months. The two tornadoes that damaged a large proportion of the coastal Sussex town of Selsey in 1998 and 2000 occurred in October and January respectively. In the former, 25 per cent of Selsey was damaged or destroyed.

Strong refers to T4 to T7 (F2–F3) and these are regularly experienced in *Tornado alley* over the Great Plains of southern USA between the Rockies and Appalachians and including the valleys of the Mississippi, Missouri and Ohio rivers. Here a special set of conditions include warm moist air from the Gulf of Mexico, a hot dry layer from the Rockies at about 3000ft (915m) and a strong easterly wind at 10,000ft (3048m). Supercell storms are induced and conflicting winds generate rotation. Within the cloud a meso-cyclone forms that moves downward as a funnel-shaped stalk. At first this may be hardly visible. When it contacts the ground it becomes dark with dust and debris. Some tornadoes develop so rapidly that there is little if any advance warning. Most occur at the rear of the supercell. It is normal for there to be an unnatural calm before the tornado hits.

The speed of movement lies somewhere between 30 and 70mph (48 and 113kph) and some tornadoes may be as much as a mile wide.

Violent tornadoes include T8 (F4-F5) and above. Such tornadoes are luckily rare. The Jefferson County Al tornado of 8 April 1998 left 30 people dead and hundreds injured. It is regarded as the most powerful tornado in history and has been categorised as F5

Tornado precautions

If you see a funnel-cloud forming, treat it as a possible tornado and act accordingly. However, many funnel-clouds never reach the ground. Funnel-clouds that reach the sea surface form waterspouts. These may be dangerous to small craft. However, spouts that are generated when a tornado leaves land for the sea (*tornado-storm spouts*) are potentially devastating. Cold air over relatively warm sea, and maybe an island or

Photo 9 A classic tornado snakes down to touch the ground in a cloud of debris (lower left horizon). The black mushroom-like cloud from which it emerges is typical of the supercells which spawn these monsters.
PHOTO: MIKE HOLLINGSHEAD

THE INTERNATIONAL TORNADO INTENSITY (T) SCALE			
Intensity	Description	Damage caused	Wind speed
T0	Light	Litter raised, trail visible through crops, twigs snapped	39–54mph (17–24m/s)
T1	Mild	Heavier litter raised, wooden fences flattened, tiles dislodged, minor shed damage	55–72mph (25–32m/s)
T2	Moderate	Trailers blown over, sheds and garage roofs destroyed, much damage to tiled roofs and chimneys, small trees uprooted	73–92mph (33–41m/s)
T3	Strong	Mobile homes overturned, garages etc. destroyed, bigger trees damaged or uprooted, some airborne debris, walls blown over, some buildings shaken	93–114mph (42–51m/s)
T4	Severe	Cars and mobile homes levitated, entire roofs removed, debris carried for a mile or more (2km), large trees uprooted and moved	115–136mph (52–61m/s)
T5	Intense	Heavier vehicles levitated, entire roofs and bricks removed, items sucked out from within houses, older buildings may collapse, telegraph poles snap	137–160mph (62–72m/s)
T6	Moderately devastating	Major damage to strong houses, bricks etc. become missiles, small structures elevated, embedded objects	161–186mph (73–83m/s)
T7	Strongly devastating	Brick and wooden-frame houses demolished, some large steel-framed structures severely damaged, much heavy flying debris	187–212mph (84–95m/s)
T8	Severely devastating	Cars carried great distances, most houses demolished, danger from heavy flying debris	213–240mph (96–107m/s)
T9	Intensely devastating	Steel-framed buildings demolished, trains hurled some distance, survival reliant on underground shelters	241–296mph (108–120m/s)

THE FUJITA SCALE (F-SCALE)
This is less scientifically based than the T-scale but is used in America.
F0 (Gale tornado) covers T0 and T1
F1 (Moderate tornado) covers T2 and T3
F2 (Significant tornado) covers T4 and T5
F3 (Severe tornado) covers T6 and T7
F4 (Devastating tornado) covers T8 and T9

other high ground to windward, can induce spouts that come ashore.

In the USA, NOAA Weather Radio will warn of tornado risk. When advancing storm clouds are dark and maybe greenish in colour you should suspect a tornado. When rain starts with heavy thunder, allow for large hailstones. Search the horizon for the characteristic funnel. When imminent, tornadoes will emit a load roar. Hopefully by this time you should be in adequate shelter, such as a specially designed underground safe room, a basement or storm cellar. If none of these are available go to the lowest level at the centre of your house, putting as many walls as possible between you and the outside. Keep clear of windows and doors, and keep them closed. If you can, get under a sturdy table.

If you are in a car or a mobile home, then abandon them in good time and find shelter in a sturdy (steel-framed if possible) building. You will be particularly vulnerable in a caravan or mobile home. Trying to dodge or outrun a tornado in a car will often not be a safe bet as tornadoes snake and change direction.

If you are outside and unable to find other shelter, lie prone in a ditch or depression but consider whether it might flood. Do not shelter in the lee of any building or wall – it may collapse on you. Avoid

Photo 10 The wreckage of a house in Moore, Oklahoma after a tornado had struck on 7 May 1990. Some 1500 homes were destroyed with 41 fatalities over the area of the outbreak. It was Oklahoma's deadliest tornado for 50 years. PHOTO COURTESY OF NOAA

sheltering under bridges or overpasses. Check if the site you have chosen is relatively safe from flying debris.

Some remarkable tornado outbreaks in the USA

The death toll from tornadoes was greatest before the 20th century as there were then no warning systems and organised evacuations. However, the deadliest outbreak of modern times occurred on 18 March 1925. The event was named the Tri-State Tornadoes, leaving 747 dead and 2,027 injured. One tornado travelled 219 miles from Ellington, Missouri to Princeton, Indiana.

The Flint (Michigan) tornado of 8 9 June 1953 was the last single tornado to kill over 100 people (115). The outbreak ran east into central Massachusetts – where a further 94 people were killed and 4,000 buildings were damaged or destroyed.

The so-called Super Outbreak of 3–4 April 1947 was when 148 tornados ravaged 13 states in the South and Midwest. Total deaths amounted to 350 and there was $600 million in damage.

Seventy tornadoes swept across Texas, Oklahoma and Kansas on 8 April 1999. This is considered to be the largest and most costly outbreak of tornadoes ever recorded with a toll of 45 dead and $1.2 billion in damage.

Severe tornadoes elsewhere

The West Coast of South Island NZ is considered a tornado hot-spot due to thunderstorms and the effect of the Southern Alps. On 10 March 2005, a 1,300ft (400m) wide tornado travelled for 2.5 miles (4.5km), devastating Greymouth and costing millions in damage. Similar events occurred in March 2001 and June 2003 and there were seven during the years 2000–2007.

Tornado frequency in Europe is far less than in the USA, which is mainly due to the barrier of the Alps. For every 30 tornadoes in Iowa there are 10 in Britain and only 2 or 3 in Austria. They are also much weaker, being largely F1 or F2 in strength.

The London tornado of 23 October 1091 is considered the earliest and strongest known British tornado, although the Southsea, Hampshire one of 14 December 1810 may rival it. The strongest European tornado is possibly the Seine-Maritime outbreak of 19 August 1845 when there were up to 200 casualties. There were more than 500 fatalities in the Sicily tornado of December 1851. Between 24–25 June 1967 there were destructive outbreaks over France, Belgium and the Netherlands with more than 15 fatalities. In 2006 there were outbreaks across Western Europe that led to two deaths and some 60 injuries.

Almost all rain starts off as snow. Clouds that extend up above the level where the temperature has fallen to around -13°C are going to form snowflakes in their higher reaches. These flakes fall and melt into raindrops. So if the surface air temperature is somewhere near freezing the flakes do not melt and we have a snowfall.

Snowflakes' shapes are an infinite variation on hexagons. This is because of the molecular make-up of the water vapour that forms them. Water molecules freeze into six-sided ice-crystals and the 'wetter' the cloud the bigger the flakes.

It may be hot and humid before summer thunderstorms but up in the storm clouds the temperatures can be down to −50°C and the snow-making processes are very strong. So enormous flakes form and melt into a multitude of very big raindrops. These so-called *thunderspots* are increased in size by being electrically charged.

Continuous snow

When warm fronts and occlusions precipitate into air that is at or below freezing at the surface we get continuous snow. Often, light rain will evaporate before it reaches the ground. When it is cold, however, many rafts of cloud that would not produce any rain when it was warmer will snow because the flakes do not melt on their way down. So predicting snowfall is a forecaster's nightmare. If it rains a bit no one cares but if there is just a little snow, people get worried.

Another way continuous snow occurs is when a cold, moist, air-stream is lifted over hill and mountain slopes. Even relatively minor undulations in the ground can induce quite heavy snow in places, while in other areas close by there is very little if any.

The heaviest falls often occur when small lows invade an area or when an occluded front becomes slow-moving. Such lows are difficult to forecast accurately.

Intermittent snow

When snow-showers appear or when layer clouds develop holes we get intermittent snow. Snow showers may seem continuous at times because the gaps in between become filled with flakes that have taken time to fall.

In winter, the sea is very often warm compared to the air above it. This is an unstable situation and snow showers erupt to bring considerable falls to coastal areas facing the wind. As they drive inland, these showers often dissipate.

The wind will often turn a moderate fall of snow into a heavy one through drifting which often leads to gridlock on the roads.

Preparing for snow

Do not be surprised if snow does not occur as forecast or there is more or less than expected. Snow is difficult to forecast in the short-term. If there is a possibility of snow, try to avoid travelling but if you have to travel then avoid minor roads if possible. Gritting and snow-clearing operations will be carried out on major routes first. Also, if you get stuck there is more chance of rescue on a major route.

If you have to make a journey, add warm clothes, boots and a spade or shovel to the gear you would normally carry in the car. Make sure your tank is well filled with petrol because, if stuck, you may need to run the engine for an extended period in order to keep warm. If you do run the engine check that the exhaust tail-pipe is kept clear of snow or you might die of carbon monoxide fumes. You will also possibly need food and water – don't forget food for the dog if it is with you.

In heavy snowfalls, motorists have been known to die through abandoning their cars and trying to reach shelter through deep drifts.

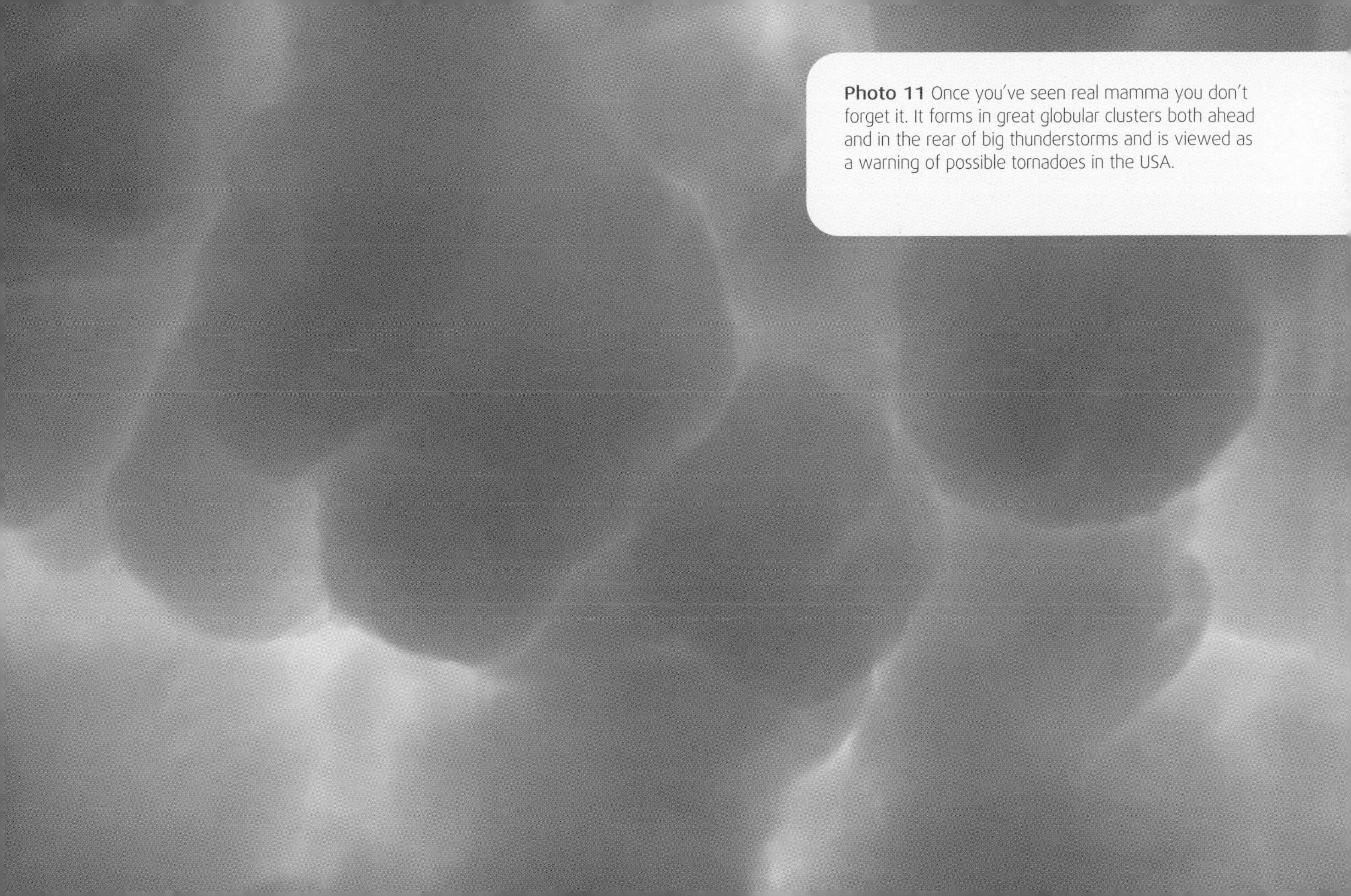

Photo 11 Once you've seen real mamma you don't forget it. It forms in great globular clusters both ahead and in the rear of big thunderstorms and is viewed as a warning of possible tornadoes in the USA.

Do this only as a last resort. In mountainous districts, assess the chance of avalanches extending across the road.

The direction you travel and the direction of the wind have a bearing on your chances of avoiding the worst effects of a snowfall. Snow tends to come in bands. If we assume that snow clouds will travel at about 30–40mph (40–60km/h) and are travelling fairly parallel to the route you have chosen, then you will (on a motorway for example) travel in the same direction, stay under them for a much longer period than if you are driving into them. On the other hand, when driving into the snow, you can add the cloud's speed to your own and so can expect a much reduced period of snowfall. However, you must expect to meet deeper snow before it clears.

If the wind is generally from the side and is brisk, closure of the road due to drifting is the major problem. Drifting snow on open stretches without much traffic produces a serious hazard.

At home, stow your shovels on the leeward side of the house. Drifts may make it impossible to open windward doors. Beware of large volumes of snow falling from roofs, especially when a thaw sets in after a period of freezing temperatures. If possible, have a supply of sand within easy reach to spread on frozen paths, drives and patios etc.

Snow at night

Overnight snowfall creates the greatest problems. Few vehicles are about to keep the roads clear and it is the time of lowest temperature. Snowfall often comes with cold fronts where the temperature plummets as the skies clear. It is a well-known effect that temperatures tend to rise before snow so any snow that fell during the previous day may have melted and frozen overnight. New snow over frozen surfaces is a great hazard, especially if the snow starts to melt with the onset of the day. So snowfall that occurs during late afternoon or early evening may well cause the biggest problems the next day due to iciness.

Heaviest snowfalls

The contours of your surroundings will have a great effect on snowfall. If you live on a hill slope that faces the wind, you will get much more snow than over the adjacent flatlands. You must expect the maximum over the crests and in the immediate lee of them but further away downwind there will be less snowfall because the hill tops have robbed the clouds of much of their snow-making potential. Living in one of these *snow-shadows*, you may be surprised to find how difficult conditions are in the surrounding areas that have not been protected by a hill top or ridge.

Heavy snowfall is not often associated with fast-moving fronts such as may occur with winter depressions. It is the slow-moving old fronts such as occlusions that usually spawn the biggest snowfall. If you see on a current weather chart that there is a front stretching more-or-less the same direction as the isobars, then allow for an extended snowfall. The same goes for small local depressions that may hardly register on a weather chart or perhaps just have a single isobar round them.

Photo 12 Supercell storms generate giant hailstones. Luckily they are not all as large as this 7 inch diameter example. Hail from normal thunderstorms is not often larger than peas but giant hail sometimes falls in Europe and is well-known in Australia.
PHOTO COURTESY OF NOAA

Photo 13 When giant snowflakes fall, there is often little wind so the clouds remain fairly stationary. The result is a rapid, deep deposit of snow – usually wet – but problems occur when it freezes overnight and dries. If a wind blows in the morning the result is deep drifts. PHOTO: SHUTTERSTOCK

When you go into mountains, or even just hills, weather conditions are not as stable as on the lowlands. Deterioration in the weather happens unexpectedly and fast; what seemed at first to be a set-fair day may prove, later, to be anything but.

To produce cloud and rain (or snow) air must ascend. It does that in hilly areas by being forced up slopes. So, when an airstream is already moist, slopes facing the wind can become shrouded in fog or mist. Drizzle can be dense and persistent, whereas on the lowlands the conditions may be cloudy but clear. On the whole, the stronger the wind, the faster the rate of ascent and the denser the rain and drizzle. In the winter, snow storms can erupt apparently out of nowhere.

It is a well-known fact that the weather on the north side of the Alps is less predictable than on the south side. In any case, the weather is very changeable; these conditions will apply to most mountain ranges in the temperate latitudes of either hemisphere.

Signs of good weather are also helpful to mountain walkers. In quiet weather *mountain winds* blow up the valleys towards the mountains during the day while *valley winds* blow down the valleys from the mountains during the night. Their persistence indicates that the quiet conditions should continue for a while at least. In these conditions, on lakes where one side is in the sun while the other is shaded, there will be *lake winds* blowing onto the sunny shores and away from the shaded shores. As the sun moves round, this regime may become neutral with neither side being favoured; later, the lake breeze may reverse direction. Unless dense cirrus banners (photo 2) begin to invade the high sky this is another sign of continuing good weather.

However, wind speeds increase with altitude and sometimes the coldest conditions accompany clear weather when the airstream has a polar origin. Then wind chill (see table on page 50) is at maximum. If the weather deteriorates and rain or snow sets in,

conditions could possibly become life-threatening unless you are very well prepared.

Temperature falls at a rate of about 1°C per 100m (300ft) on average but sometimes it is less and sometimes more, depending on the conditions.

At low altitude the wind direction is guided by valleys. The usual height of cumulus clouds is 2000–3000ft (600–900m) and their motion can determine true wind direction for mountains and hills lower than this. With higher peaks, snow plumes blowing off summits can be used as indicators of wind direction. Clouds higher than cumulus may not be reliable guides as they often move at angles to the true surface wind, especially when the weather is on the change.

Changes in barometric pressure

Even if you are not planning to go very high, an altimeter designed for climbers is very helpful. An altimeter is basically a barometer and so can be used in forecasting the immediate weather. Here are a few pointers.

Falling pressure

A lengthy period of continuously falling pressure indicates an equally extended period of rain (or snow). Wind should also shift into the southern quadrants to be followed later by shifts towards west or northwest (NH).

If the fall is rapid, expect wind and heavy rain (or snow) soon. Also, low cloud will create hill fog.

Thunderstorms often follow sharp falls of pressure when conditions are already warm and humid. Winds are often light.

In settled weather, small falls in the afternoons, especially in summer, have little forecasting value. However, a rise that occurs only in the afternoon points to deteriorating conditions.

Photo 14 Storms that build up in mountainous districts will often show themselves over the summits first. Here the Eiger in the Bernese Alps, topping 3970m (13,125ft) high, shows signs of approaching storms with the veil of cirrus clouds above. Low cloud can be seen invading the slopes on the extreme left, so expect deterioration very soon. PHOTO: INGE MOORE

Rising pressure

If weather is already fine and pressure rises sharply do not expect the fine weather to last for long.

A rapid rise leads to fine weather but it often only lasts as long as the period of the rise.

A slow rise over several days indicates the onset of an extended period of settled weather. This is more likely if, at the same time, the wind veers from the southern into the northern quadrant (NH).

Allow for fog or mist when high pressure is accompanied by high humidity.

If the pressure changes erratically then expect unsettled weather.

Forward planning

Even if the morning weather is fine, have you allowed for deterioration? Have you checked the local forecast?

If you are going hill walking or climbing, make sure you have adequate clothing in your backpack. Take energy-giving foods such as chocolate. Avoid fatty and meaty foods but steep walking or climbing leads to sweating, so salt intake is essential. Fruit juices are preferable to plain water.

Get local advice on your proposed route; if you haven't done it before, check if there are any extra hazards. If the weather suddenly closes in, will you know the route well enough to safely return to lower ground? What are the risks of avalanches? See pages 44–5.

UV light is stronger at altitude so take sunglasses with side protection and plenty of high-factor sun cream for exposed skin, especially lips. Some form of hat is essential on sunny days at altitude.

Showers and thunderstorms

These can provide some very testing conditions for hill-walkers. Warm summer mornings can entice people to go walking in the hills and mountains without adequate protection. Storms may easily break out in the afternoon following a fine, warm morning. Keep an eye out for heap clouds (photo 15); if you can see them growing so that their depth is considerably greater than the distance from bases to ground level, then expect showers or possibly thunderstorms. They may not arrive but you should be prepared for them. If you get caught in a storm on a mountain then follow the advice given on page 26. You may get very wet but hopefully will be protected from a lightning strike.

MOUNTAIN WEATHER PATTERNS	
Signs to look for	Expect
High clouds (cirrus) moving in (usually from some point west) and increasing	Bad weather in next 5–15 hours
Solar haloes ie slightly coloured rings about sun or moon	Bad weather in next 4–12 hours
Lowering cloud forming over neighbouring tops or ridges. Sudden appearance of wraiths of mist blowing down slopes to windward	Sudden clamps of hill fog, drizzle, rain or snow imminent
Heap clouds – if these are about in the morning	Allow for growth into showers later
Heap clouds – large	Showers very probable with possible thunder
Medium-level clouds showing many lens-shaped elements	Any rain etc may well be delayed
Clearance into blue sky from high overcast (rain etc stopped some time ago). Now cooler. Excellent visibility	Allow for further showers to follow fair period. Further outlook – fair

Photo 15 Walkers on lesser mountain ranges are possibly more at risk from sudden weather deteriorations because the signs may not be so evident. Although the skies above are clear, not far away heavy thunderstorms cover the mountain tops

11 Avalanches

More than a million avalanches occur in the world each year. In a typical year, avalanches claim the lives of over 150 people worldwide and, because of the increase in mountain tourism, this number is increasing. Commercial leisure enterprises may lead to development in zones possibly prone to avalanches. If you know a little about the vagaries of snow and are careful to assess the possible dangers, you can avoid being one of the casualties. However, avalanches are a potential hazard whenever there has been a heavy snowfall, especially after there have been previous snowfalls.

Because snow is frozen water it can weigh a great deal. A cubic metre (35 cubic feet) of freshly fallen *powder snow* weighs somewhere between 30 and 60kg (66–132lb). However, if the temperature during the snowfall is not far from freezing then it will be *wet snow* and will then weigh more. After a lapse of some 24 hours the composition of the newly fallen snow will change due to atmospheric conditions and also internally because of its own weight. It compacts and can then weigh anything between 200 and 600kg (440–1300lb). As it settles it may transform into what is called *firn snow*. It becomes granulated and the granulations become firmly frozen together. Wet *firn snow* can weigh as much as half a ton per cubic metre. This effect is induced by the sun and so firn snow will be found on the sunlit sides, whereas on the shaded sides the snow may still be powder.

Avalanches may be started by people venturing onto snow surfaces that are already unstable. They can also be triggered by loud noise or can suddenly occur for no apparent reason.

Caught in an avalanche

If the snow is powder think of it as a liquid. Throw off skis and backpack. Try 'swimming' upwards to keep near the top of the snow. If you become trapped, try to keep an air-pocket in front of your face using your hands and arms. Expand your chest. If you don't, you may suffocate as, within a few seconds of the snow ceasing to run, it will set hard. You may become disorientated. Which direction is up? Remember everything falls down due to gravity so you can find which way is down by spitting.

Your chances of survival are enhanced if you do not panic. Breathe steadily and remain calm to conserve energy. Try not to shout until you are aware of someone near you. Snow suppresses sound and, unless you are already near the surface, it will only carry a short distance.

Your chances of rescue will be improved if you tell someone where you are going. However, this will only be useful if you stick to your plan.

Avoiding avalanches

Listen to weather forecasts and do not venture out if sudden changes in the weather appear imminent. If a föhn is blowing, delay leaving until all risk has passed. Do not go out immediately after a fall of new snow.

Do not set foot on steep lee slopes, especially when weather is changeable. South-facing slopes can be very dangerous in strong sunshine but safer in the early morning and later when fully shaded.

Photo 16 When slopes are as steep as this, avalanches are inevitable and will cause hazards on lower, lesser slopes. PHOTO: SHUTTERSTOCK

Avalanches

Ask local experts about the conditions, including foresters and wood cutters, as well as snow professionals such as hut guardians. It requires long experience to assess avalanche risks in any locality and you should always consult those people whose lives and livelihoods depend on their knowledge.

Piste skiing hazards

Whilst you need to assess the risk of avalanches when traversing snow fields, there are also inherent dangers in piste skiing. Research has shown that 20 per cent of ski injuries are caused by going too fast. This percentage is almost equalled by skiing on wet snow, while a smaller number of accidents occur in deep virgin snow and through encountering icy patches. The rest – the highest percentage – are due to inexperience on skis.

While pistes will be sited to minimise the risk of avalanches, they can occur on pistes and the risk may not always be recognised by those in charge of safety. Learn about snow conditions and keep your own weather-eye open.

In the period from 1988–99, Austria had 56 avalanches with 50 deaths and 70 significant injuries. In the worst incident, which occurred over the Christmas period of 1999, nine German tourists died with just one survivor rescued by helicopter. In addition, the avalanches levelled millions of trees.

FACTORS THAT AFFECT AVALANCHES		
Aspect	Effect on potential risk	Comments
Weather	Highest during or within 24 hours of snowfall of about a foot in depth	If there has been heavy snowfall postpone your trip. Below 6in: low risk
Snowfall	New snow may not bond to existing snow layer	New deep layers may lead to blockage of roads and major destruction
Temperature	Passage of warm fronts cause long-term melting in the snowpack and increased risk	Spring snow conditions with daytime melting and night-time freezing can help stabilise and lower risk
Wind	Scours snow from windward side and drops it on leeward	Higher risk on leeward side where ski areas are often sited. So travel on windward side
Snowpack	Previous invisible falls can lead to instability down to several feet below the surface	Ask the locals about the season's history. Snow stability can change during a single day
Slope angle	Highest risk when slope lies between 30° and 45°	Allow for varying angles of a slope. Wet snow can run at lesser angles
Slope orientation	Most runs occur when slopes face between N and E	Can run down slopes facing any direction. Avoid slopes that remain shadowed during the day
Terrain	Suspect bowls and gullies higher up. Avoid crossing them lower down, even if they are apparently quite minor	If possible, avoid crossing steep slopes or valley floors with deep snow above. Assess whether the roads you will use are at risk

Photo 17 Strong waterspouts like this can be dangerous to small craft. Also, near the coast they may be tornado storm spouts. PHOTO: SHUTTERSTOCK

Major flooding anywhere is due to excessive rainfall and/or a sudden thaw. Close to a coastline it may be due to excessively high tides – a tidal surge – or there could be a flash flood when heavy rain storms occur over coastal foothills. Local flash floods can occur anywhere in hilly or mountainous districts where streams or rivers are forced into narrow channels by the terrain.

A number of major floods have become well-remembered. In 1990, a million square kilometres of land in Eastern Australia were submerged. Then there were the Mississippi floods of 1993. Floods covered large swathes of Central England in 2007, but were not nearly as devastating as the great European floods of August 2002.

The latter were caused by a certain set of circumstances: continuous rain must be due to steady and prolonged lifting of moist air. The air came from the Mediterranean region and was very humid; high ground in the path of the wind lifted the air and this was aided by a virtually stationary front. The rivers Elbe and Danube swelled to heights unseen for 100 years so vast areas of the Czech Republic, eastern Germany, Austria and Hungary were flooded. Often thunderstorms over high ground produce torrents but in this case there were hardly any thunderstorms.

It is not the travelling depressions that produce the worst effects. If depressions move then their fronts go with them but, while the rain may be temporarily heavy, it does move on. It is when the front becomes detached from the low with which it formed, and is almost stationary, while being fed by two airmasses of different temperatures and humidities, that produces conditions for widespread flooding.

The increased incidence of flooding in Europe during the millennium years has meant that the warning systems are now better than they were. Satellite images can observe the extent of the flooded areas and so – almost in real time – enable many authorities to pin-point the problem areas and take steps to mitigate the worst effects. If you go to places which have habitual monsoons (eg the Indian subcontinent and south east Asia as well as some of Australasia) then check beforehand when the rainy season is and, if possible, where the worst effects are usually felt. Bangladesh is one of the worst affected areas and catastrophic floods are endemic there. However, the worst coastal flooding is generally due to cyclones producing tidal surges.

Flash floods

These are more of a hazard as they are localised and do not conform to any pattern. They are also more likely to occur in the summer than in the winter; typically down the coombes and gulleys that lead hill water to the sea. A devastating flash flood struck the north Cornish fishing village of Boscastle beneath Bodmin Moor, on 16 August 2004. This occurred 50 years to the day after a similar disaster at Lynmouth in Devon on 15–16 August 1952, which claimed 37 lives.

Precautions

If you camp by a hill stream always assess the chances of a flash flood and consider moving to higher ground if storms are occurring inland. The same goes for lakesides especially when the land rises steeply away from the lake.

Unless they are already happening or forecast, you cannot expect to know about impending widespread floods such as occurred in central Europe in 2004. So you need to consider if you may be at risk if you are on a possible flood-plain. It would appear that flooding is now becoming a greater problem as more and more building takes place on what are known to be flood plains.

Photo 18 This is what can happen to your car if it is caught up in flash floods, or when rivers burst their banks. The heaviest and most prolonged rainfall is often over higher ground which may be some distance from where serious floods occur. PHOTO: SHUTTERSTOCK

13 Deep cold and ice storms

The definition of 'cold' depends on where you live because we acclimatise to our local temperature and, if we live in areas subject to severe winters, we make provision for very cold weather. So people who live in Canada, Scandinavia and Northern Russia, for example, will be less likely to suffer from the effects of cold winters because they are used to coping with them. Even so, there are conditions so stringent that even local inhabitants will find them life-threatening.

Wind chill

When air temperatures are low, then wind chill will make the air feel much colder. The following table shows the decrease in air temperature due to the wind chill factor. This means that the risk of frostbite is heightened with increasing wind.

This is the Wind Chill Chart used in Canada; all others will be much the same but measured in different units.

WIND CHILL CHART – TEMPERATURE (°C)/WIND SPEED (km/h)												
mph* km/h		5°C	0°C	-5°C	-10°C	-15°C	-20°C	-25°C	-30°C	-35°C	-40°C	-45°C
3	5	4	-2	-7	-13	-19	-24	-30	-36	-41	-47	-53
6 (2)	10	3	-3	-9	-15	-21	-27	-33	-39	-45	-51	-57
9	15	2	-4	-11	-17	-23	-29	-35	-41	-48	-54	-60
12 (3)	20	1	-5	-12	-18	-24	-30	-37	-43	-49	-56	-62
16	25	1	-6	-12	-19	-25	-32	-38	-44	-51	-57	-64
19 (4)	30	0	-6	-13	-20	-26	-33	-39	-46	-52	-59	-65
22	35	0	-7	-14	-20	-27	-33	-40	-47	-53	-60	-66
25 (5)	40	-1	-7	-14	-21	-27	-34	-41	-48	-54	-61	-68
28	45	-1	-8	-15	-21	-28	-35	-42	-48	-55	-62	-69
31 (6)	50	-2	-8	-15	-22	-29	-35	-42	-49	-56	-63	-69
34	55	-2	-8	-15	-22	-29	-36	-43	-50	-57	-63	-70
37 (7)	60	-2	-9	-16	-23	-30	-36	-43	-50	-57	-64	-71
40	65	-2	9	-16	-23	-30	-37	-44	-51	-58	-65	-72
44 (8)	70	-2	-9	-16	-23	-30	-37	-44	-51	-58	-65	-72
47	75	-3	10	-17	-24	-31	-38	-45	-52	-59	-66	-73
50	80	-3	-10	-17	-24	-31	-38	-45	-52	-60	-67	-74

* Beaufort Force given in brackets

General precautions in very cold weather

The forecasts will usually warn of very cold weather so dress accordingly. Sub-layers of loose-fitting clothes will trap body heat and aid air circulation. Outer garments must be waterproof and tightly woven with a hood or balaclava. Some kind of headgear is essential and, when it is very cold, tie a woolly scarf around your mouth. Mittens are considered warmer than gloves – and more practical.

If you have to take a car journey, check your antifreeze level and observe the precautions given on page 36-8 (Snowstorms). If you have children or elderly people with you, make particularly sure they are well provided for. If your engine breaks down, or you have to change a wheel, remember that strenuous outdoor activity in cold weather puts a strain on the heart. Is there a risk of frostbite? Even if it doesn't seem very cold, there may be danger from hypothermia. A prolonged period of cold will lower body temperature, leading to shivering, confusion and loss of muscular control. If these symptoms occur, wrap the patient in any available material to conserve heat and seek medical attention immediately as unconsciousness and death could follow. Do not give alcohol.

Photo 19 The dramatic effects of an ice storm over Lake Geneva (Lake Leman) on 26 January 2005 when winds gusted to 65kts (110km/hr) and temperatures dropped to sub-zero. Some craft on the lake sank due to the weight of ice. PHOTO J-P SCHERRER

At home do you have any means of keeping warm if the power goes off? Do you have a bottled gas heater, cooking and water-heating facilities? If you have an open fire do you have sufficient fuel for it within easy reach? Don't leave the provision of these essentials until the cold weather arrives – everyone else will be stocking up.

If there is heavy snow, keep a shovel indoors to dig a way out on the leeward side of the house; you may not be able to get out of the windward side.

Freezing rain may bring down overhead power cables. The local lines feeding power to your house are likely to be the first to go but a universal black-out will follow if the grid lines come down, often taking the towers with them. When that happens, it may take days, or even weeks, for you to be re-connected.

So if the period of deep cold continues, and you have no power, you may need to abandon the house. If it should come to that, turn off the water supply to the house as well as the electricity, which might come on again when you are not there. Drain immersion tanks. Turn on taps to empty them of accumulated water. Consult the frost-protection advice in the operating manuals for washing machines, dishwashers and the central heating system.

A light glazed frost won't cause much damage to trees, but a heavier one may bring down whole large branches and split trunks; so, where possible, avoid being close to trees. The ice storm of 6 January 1998, which affected Southern Quebec, Eastern Ontario and Northern New England, was the worst in the area in living memory. A million homes were left without power; bridges and roads were closed; shelters for people forced to abandon their homes were set up, and shops and restaurants had to close because staff could not get to work. In addition, almost all the trees in Montreal suffered damage and some were even destroyed by the extreme cold.

Why do we get freezing rain?

In most places in the temperate latitudes, freezing rain leading to a glazed frost is a rare occurrence. North America is one area that can be affected and the conditions occur just ahead of warm fronts or occlusions which are advancing over icy-cold surfaces. There must be a warmer air layer (above freezing) at a moderate altitude, with snow falling into it from higher up. The snow melts into raindrops which are close to freezing. On striking the frozen ground, the super-cooled water drops spread and immediately freeze. So branches, leaves, pavements, roads, railings all become encased in ice which makes walking or driving practically impossible. If the rain continues or drizzle increases, the encasing ice and an ice storm is the result (see photo 19). Luckily, glazed frosts, which are never severe enough to be classed as ice storms, are very rare in temperate latitudes.

When does the sea freeze?

Sea water will only freeze when the air temperature falls several degrees below freezing point. So it is rare for the sea to freeze on the coasts of Atlantic Europe, except in Scandinavia where the Baltic freezes every winter. However, in tidal creeks, when low water happens to coincide with a winter night under clear skies, the drying shores and banks can fall well below freezing before the next flood tide. The edge-water then freezes and if the cold snap is prolonged, extensive ice floes can build up (photo 20). Under these circumstances, wooden craft left on moorings will be subject to damage along their waterlines and glassfibre hulls will probably need repair. Metal fittings such as stanchions and pulpits will be much colder than the seawater, and spray will build up as a potentially dangerous top heavy coating of ice.

Photo 20 The weather has to be exceptionally cold for the sea to freeze in temperate latitudes, but it does occur occasionally. These ice floes appeared around all the creeks of the east and south coasts of England (and elsewhere) in the big freeze of 1963. Boats may not be crushed but they can suffer damage to their hulls.

14 Falling and mountain winds

Wherever there are mountains there will be local winds. These appear fairly regularly and are due primarily to katabatic effects: cold air, being dense, will sink down the valleys. If these falling winds are in much the same direction as the wind caused by the local pressure pattern, they can become strong or even gale-force, especially where the valleys constrict them. They can be cold but often they are warm and dry because air that sinks warms up and much of its moisture has been deposited on the other side of the mountains. A falling wind can bring psychological and other problems with it. It can, in coastal districts, reverse the normal pattern of the strongest wind occurring in the middle of the day and least in the early morning. The bora of the Adriatic is like that. The mistral of the Rhône Valley is so-called because of the masterful way it takes over and sweeps away other lesser winds (photo 21).

Wind name	Region	Comments
Europe		
Alm	Karst region (Trieste)	Falling wind
Autan	Corbieres Mountains, S France	Hot, dry falling wind
Bora	North-east Adriatic coast	Dry, cold NE wind off Dinaric Alps
Drinet	Rumania	Cold, mountain wind
Föhn	Alpine foreland	Warm, dry falling wind
Halmiak	Croatian coast	Falling wind
Ibe	Caucasus	Falling wind
Jura	Foothills of Jura	Cold, gusty mountain wind

Wind name	Region	Comments
Maestrale	Gulf of Genoa	Dry, cold, gale-force Mistral type in winter
Maledetto	Northern Italy	Falling wind
Matiniere	Alps	Sometimes violent mountain wind
Melamboreas	Provence	Northerly mistral-type wind
Mistral	Rhône Valley	Strong down-slope wind. Felt over much of north shores of Gulf of Lions. Sometimes gale-force
Piterak	Iceland/Greenland	Severe falling wind down fjords. Gusts of up to 140kt
Pyr (Pyrn)	Upper Danube	Falling wind
Riesenbirg	Germany	Falling wind
Roeteturm	Rumania	Falling wind
Tramontana	Italy	Strong, cold mountain wind
Vaudaire	Lake Geneva	Local name for föhn
Vent d'Espagne	Pyrenees	Föhn-type blowing into southern France
Americas		
Chinook	Lee of Rockies	Hot, dry falling wind – the 'Snow Eater' especially Montana
Coho	Oregon	Like Bora, up to 80mph in Portland area
Easter	Oregon	Falling wind
Santa Ana	Southern California	NE falling wind
Surazo	Peruvian Andes	Strong, cold mountain wind
Southern Hemisphere		
Berg	South Africa	Hot, dry falling wind
Nor'wester	Christchurch, New Zealand	Falling wind

Photo 21 The mistral of the Rhône Valley in southern France sometimes blows at gale or even severe gale force. It is a falling wind coming from higher ground inland which can arise in all seasons and across the whole of the Mediterranean coast of France.
PHOTO: SHUTTERSTOCK

15 Bad weather winds of the world

All over the world there are winds that bring bad weather of various types to different localities. The following list is not exhaustive but includes strong to gale force winds, sand and dust storms, blizzards etc to limited areas. These do not include the down-slope, mountain and falling winds which are listed on page 60.

Wind name	Region	Comments
Europe		
Auster	West and central Europe	Heat waves, haze, thunderstorms. Spring and autumn
Astru	Austria/Hungary	Very cold winter wind
Bise	Languedoc, France	Cold, dry NE wind. Often very overcast
Cantalaise	Aubrac plateau, France	Violent wind with snow
Cierco	Ebro region, Spain	Cold, westerly Mistral outflow
Crivetz	Rumania	Cold, strong NE wind, blizzards
Elvegast	Norway	Cold, dry easterly
Gallerna	Bay of Biscay	Cold, squally northwesterly. Gusts to 60kt
Helm	Cumberland, England	Strong NE over Pennines
Iseran	French alps	Cold, gusty northerly wind
Polack	Sudetenland	Cold, dry wind
Poriaz	Bosphorus	Violent, NE, snow in winter
Steppenwind	Germany	Cold, north-easterly wind
Wisper	Rhine Valley	Very strong evening wind through narrow constrictions

Wind name	Region	Comments
Mediterranean		
Euroclydon	Eastern Med	NE, blustery gale
Gregale	Central Med	Strong NE wind in autumn
Levanter	Balearic Islands	Easterly wind from July to October
Levanter	Straits of Gibraltar	Easterly, funnelled wind from July to October
Leveche	Southern Spain	Hot, dry, SE, dust and sand-laden
Maestral	Gulf of Genoa	Cold, strong northerly wind
Marin	Southern France	SE, moist and oppressive, with heavy rain
Meltemi	Aegean Sea	NE autumn winds
Scirroco	Much of Med	SE off Sahara mainly in spring. 'Hot evil wind'
North Africa		
Chili	Tunisia	Hot, dry southerly with sandstorms
Gergui	Algeria	Hot, dry SE wind with sandstorms
Ghibli	Tunisia	Desert wind, said to produce nervous condition of ghiblitis
Haboob	Sudan/Egypt	Dust storms, May to September
Harmattan	West African coast	Dry, dusty NE, December to February; dust blown far into Atlantic
Khamsin	Egypt	Hot, dusty scirroco-type. March to May
Middle East		
Belat	Gulf of Aden	N–NW, Dec to March, gale-force at times
Cowshee	Persian Gulf	Gusty, squally, thunderstorms in winter
Samiel	Turkey	Hot, dry, suffocating. 'Poison wind'
Sharav	Israel	Hot, dry, desert wind
Suhaili	Persian Gulf	Strong, cold SW wind

Wind name	Region	Comments
Southeast Asia and Far East		
Arashi	Japan	A storm wind
Challiho	India	Strong S wind preceding SW monsoon
Karaburan	Gobi desert	The 'black' ENE wind. Cold with dust storms
Australasia		
Buster (Burster)	Southwest Australia	An eerie lull, then cold, wet southerly wind
Southerly Buster	Sydney	Strong, cooling, coastal evening wind
Willy-Willy	Timor Sea	Tropical storm
North America		
Barber	Midwest Canada and USA	Ices up beards and hair
Blue Norther	Great Plains	Strong northerly, blue-black sky. After cold front big drop in temp
Chubasco	Gulf of California and coast of Mexico	Violent short-lived gales, May to November
Norther	Texas	Influx of strong polar air preceded by warm, moist air from south
Tehuantepecer	Mexico	Cold strong northerly of Mistral type

Photo 22 (page 59) The Earth and the Moon photographed over northern South America from one of the several meteorological geostationary satellites that are strung out round the Equator. These satellites provide the half-hourly images that are seen on TV weather presentations. Here it is late summer in the northern hemisphere (NH) with the intertropical front seen like a coronet just into the southern hemisphere (SH). The storm clouds are mainly in the NH with a big concentration over northern seas. The clouds are bright because they are high-level ice crystal clouds above the storm systems. Mostly clouds move eastwards around the globe but, against this trend, hurricanes move mainly north-westwards and we see some of them as bright white dots around the Yucatan Peninsula and even in the Pacific.

The Moon has also been shown to play its part in shaping the weather because of tidal effects, not only in the oceans, but also in the surrounding atmosphere. When the strongest winds combine with a pressure pattern that affects the sea for a period measured in days, then storm surges occur. Tides do not flow out and low pressure allows the sea surface to rise. If this occurs at the time of spring tides, the combined result is exceptionally high tides. The waves batter and breach sea defences sometimes causing much destruction and even deaths.

Down near the Earth's surface, the changes in temperature, wind, humidity, etc that cause the weather and the winds that we experience lead to effects on a global scale such as El Niño and El Niña as well as tropical revolving storms. They lead to the constantly changing weather of the temperature latitudes and the almost constantly settled weather of the doldrums. Yet, it is often local conditions that rule our lives. However, today, with our greater understanding and more accurate forecasting, our chances of avoiding the worst effects of weather have never been better.

Peru's coastal desert is considered to be one of the most arid areas in the world. In 1925, there was so much rain that it carried away the railway bridge over the Rio Moche, effectively cutting off Trujillo from Lima. In 1972, flash floods closed all the northern highways, demolished houses and choked the irrigation systems with silt. We now know the reason for the flooding – these were El Niño years.

Because of the south-east trade winds (see page 7), the Pacific Ocean between South America and Australasia experiences the biggest seiche of all. It pushes the water away from America which lowers the sea level there and builds it up in the region of Indonesia. So long as the trades blow strongly, this 'slope' in the Pacific is maintained. However, every few years the trades fail and the pent-up water in the west flows back to the coasts of the Americas. The failure of the trade winds has another far-reaching effect. When the trades blow cold water from the deep Pacific upwells along the Peruvian and adjacent coasts, the waters become rich with marine life. When the trades fail, this natural harvest from the sea also fails. The waters along the coast may rise in temperature by as much as 5°C and the fish die due to lack of nutrients. As this event, catastrophic to people relying on the fish for their livelihood, peaks around late December, the Peruvian people, predominantly Catholic, associated it with Christmas, so it became known as El Niño (Christ Child). However, in the intervening period between El Niños (roughly half as frequently) the opposite occurs and the waters become cold; this phase is known as La Niña (Little Girl).

When the air pressures in both Tahiti and Darwin are compared over a period of years, it is found that there is a recurrent difference which goes from positive (Tahiti greater than Darwin) to negative (Tahiti less than Darwin). This is known as the Southern Oscillation (SO). When Tahiti air pressure is less than Darwin, those are the El Niño years. Conversely, Tahiti air pressure is greater than Darwin in La Niña years. As they are inseparable, El Niño/La Niña and the Southern Oscillation are referred to as ENSO. In the 80 or so years following 1925 the strong El Niño and La Niña (bracketed) years are as follows: 1925 (1928) 1930 1932 (1938) 1939 1941 (1950) 1951 1953 (1955) 1957 (1964) 1965 1969 (1970) 1972 (1973) 1976 1982 1986 (1988) 1991 1994 (1995) 1997 1999 (2000) 2006.

The Effect of ENSO

The usual effect of a strong El Niño is to reverse the normal seasonal trends across a wide area of the world. The high sea temperatures lead to massive thunderstorms that transport heat to high altitudes and distort the jetstreams. This major event near the Equator can affect the weather much further north. For example, rainfall in the Mediterranean has been shown to increase in El Niño (EN) years. An episode of EN may last from 12 to 18 months. The effects of La Niña tend to be the opposite of EN.

In general, the risk of natural disasters is lowest before EN appears and strongest during and after. The 1991–92 EN was responsible for the worst drought in Southern Africa for a century, affecting some 100 million people. When, due to drought, forest fires erupt then problems with smoke inhalation become endemic. Conversely, when unusual rainfall produces areas of stagnant water, malaria epidemics result. In some Pacific islands cases of dengue fever increase during EN events.

ENSO forecasts

These are the subject of much research and may be issued in general terms several seasons ahead. They become more certain some months ahead and, as signs of EN events tend to take time to develop, so positive early warning becomes possible. When visiting high-risk areas, it is advisable to go in the period before an EN is likely rather than to go when you think the maximum effect of the event has passed.

El Niño

EFFECT OF ENSO		
Region	During EN	Comments
NW South America (Peru, Ecuador, Columbia etc)	Heavy rains and floods. Malaria epidemics	Major EN events become centred on the Galapagos Islands. Loss of sea life when seas become warm. These regions are normally arid
Mexico, Arizona, New Mexico, Brazil	Normally drier	Droughts, forest fires
Southern Africa	Drought and famine	Droughts can be prolonged (years)
India, Indian Ocean SE Asia	Monsoon fails or is weak	Great thunderstorms over Indonesia move east into Central Pacific. Jetstreams are distorted. Heavy rainfall in NE India but forest fires in dry NW
NW Pacific, China Sea	Fewer typhoons	Typhoons may be weaker than in normal years
Southern north Atlantic	Fewer hurricanes	Leads to a normally weaker season
Gulf Coast States, southern and central California	More storms and heavy rainfall	Storms can be severe and appear in unusual areas

Region	During EN	Comments
US Pacific NW and northern states	Drier fall and winter	Mild over western Canada
Great Plains and upper mid-west of USA	Warmer winters	Amongst other effects warm winters decrease winter sports activities. Also there are large savings on heating bills in the USAN and E Australia Long dry periods During winter, spring and early summer. During La Niña there are heavy rains and flooding
Western Mediterranean	Increased rainfall	The increase comes in the autumn before EN but decreases in the following spring
Western Europe	Increased rainfall	The effect of El Niño and La Niña on weather in Europe will take years to become fully established

Photo 23 'Red sky in the morning, shepherd's warning' says the weather lore. Why? Because when the rising sun illuminates layers of high cloud, which are likely to be those of a warm front approaching from the west – rain and wind will probably follow during the day.

In areas such as the Mediterranean, the Middle East and the tropics we can generally expect temperatures to go close to or above blood heat (37°C or 98.6°F) during the summer. In these circumstances, even locals who are acclimatised have to rest during the heat of the day to avoid heat-stroke, when the body seriously overheats. Sun-stroke occurs at lower temperatures after prolonged exposure to direct sunshine, especially to the unprotected head and the nape of the neck; this can be a hazard during months when the sun is high in the sky. In the tropics that means every month.

You may think that sea breezes over coastal districts would be beneficial, but they can be a hazard in that they cool your body and make you forget that the sun is still very intense.

Places that are normally temperate can experience deadly heat conditions. In the Parisian heatwave of August 2003, hundreds of people died from heat-related causes. In 1995, 700 people died in Chicago from causes related to excessive heat. Towns often become the hottest areas and many medical conditions, which can normally be tolerated, become life-threatening. In August 2007 an unprecedented heatwave struck the Eastern Mediterranean, the Balkans and the Middle East. Temperatures in Bulgaria were over 40°C while in Greece and Israel they rose as high as 46°C (115°F).

Taking precautions in hot weather

During a heatwave, make sure you drink extra fluids during the day and night to allow for loss through sweating. It is dehydration during a 24 hour period that leads to illness and, if repeated over several days and nights, can lead to death. Reduce your alcohol intake as this dehydrates your body, but eat normal meals. If you have to do physical work or exercise, slow down if you begin to feel nauseous.

Take a long siesta if it is the local custom. Don't siesta by lying in the sun on a beach in case you fall asleep and get sunburnt. Keep windows closed and blinds drawn during the heat of the day but allow the cooler night air to circulate through the house.

Protection against sunburn

The spectrum of sunlight includes ultraviolet (UV) of relatively short wavelength. The shorter the wavelength, the greater its penetrating power and so the invisible UV results in skin damage which can lead to skin cancer. Gaining a tan slowly can give protection against sunburn as melanin is produced in the skin by the sun which acts as a natural UV barrier. All skin types need protection but some are very prone to sunburn. The International UV index (above) has been formulated to advise people how to protect themselves from harmful solar radiation.

INTERNATIONAL UV INDEX		
UV Index description	**Media graphic colour**	**Recommended protection**
0–2 Low danger to average person	Green	Wear sunglasses, use sunscreen if you have very fair skin
3–5 Moderate risk from unprotected sun exposure	Yellow	Wear sunglasses, use sunscreen, wear clothing and a hat. Seek shade when sun is most intense
6–7 High risk from unprotected sun	Orange	Use SPF 15 sunscreen or higher, keep out of the sun 2 hours before to 3 hours after local noon
8–10 Very high risk	Reddish purple	As above but take extra care
11+ Extreme risk	Violet	Take all precautions as above. Wear protective clothing on all exposed areas of skin. Stay in the shade

Photo 24 In the world's oldest desert, the Namib in Namibia and southwest Angola, temperatures can plummet to 0°C and rise to 50°C. So if you are travelling in areas such as these, extreme precautions need to be taken to allow for both intense heat and cold. Modern climatic conditions, such as lower rainfall and sandstorms, are causing many of the world's deserts to spread into formerly arable areas.
PHOTO: SHUTTERSTOCK

Index

air masses 5
Alm 54
altocumulus 6
altostratus 18
altostratus 6
anticyclone 7, 11
anvil cloud 23
Arashi 57
Astru 56
Auster 56
Autan 54
avalanches 44-6

bad weather systems 9
bad weather winds 56
ball lightning 26
Barber 57
barometer 13-14
barometric pressure, changes in 40
Beaufort Scale 13
Belat 56
Berg 54
Bernese Alps 41
Bise 56
blocking highs 7, 11
Blue Norther 57
Bora 54
Buster 57

camping 18
Cantalaise 56
cells, storm 20, 21
Challiho 57
Chili 56
Chinook 54
Chubasco 57
Cierco 56
cirrostratus 6, 18
cirrus 6, 16, 18
clouds 6, 42
Coho 54

col 12
cold weather precautions 50
Continental Polar air 5
convection 5
conversions, 6
Cowshee 56
Crivetz 56
cumulonimbus 9
cumulus 6
cyclones 10, 28, 30, 31

deep cold 50-3
depressions 9, 10-12, 13, 14
desert 63
Drinet 54

Earth satellite image 57, 58
Easter 54
Eiger 41
El Nino 58-60
electric storms 10
electric winds 24
Elvegast 56
ENSO 58
Euroclydon 56
evacuation 31

falling pressure 40
falling winds 54
filling-up 11
flash floods 48
floods 48-9
forecasts 16
forked lightning 26
freezing rain 52
frontal trough 12
fronts 9, 10-11, 14
frost 52
Fujita Scale 34

gale 12, 16-18
gale precautions 18
Gallerna 56

Gergui 56
Ghibli 56
Gregale 56

Haboob 56
hailstones 38
Halmiak 54
haloes 42
Harmattan 56
heap clouds 6, 42
Helm 56
high clouds 42
high level clouds 6
high pressure ridges 7, 11, 12
hot weather 62
humidity 5
Hurricane Andrew 28-9
Hurricane Katrina 30
hurricanes 28, 30

Ibe 54
ice storms 50-3
insurance 31
intense heat 62
International Tornado Intensity Scale 34
Iseran 56
isobars 11, 14

jet cirrus 16
jetstreams 5, 16
Jura 54

Karaburan 57
Khamsin 56

La Nina 58
Lake Geneva ice storm 51
lake winds 40
land breezes 8
latent heat 5, 9

layer clouds 6
Levanter 56
Leveche 56
lightning 20, 24-6
low clouds 6
low pressure 7
lowering cloud 42

Maestral 56
Maestrale 54
Maledetto 54
Marin 56
maritime Polar air 5
Matiniere 54
medium-level clouds 42
Melamboreas 54
Meltemi 56
Mistral 54, 55
monsoons 7-8, 10
Moon satellite image 57, 58
mountain 8
    lightning 26
    storms 40-3
    weather patterns 42
    winds 54
multiple cell storms 20

Namib desert 63
nimbostratus 18
NOAA 34
Nor'wester 54
Norther 57
Northern Hemisphere winds 8

occlusions 5, 9, 11
Oklahoma tornado 35

Pacific Ocean 58
Piterak 54
point action 24
Polack 56

Polar air 5, 8
Polar front 10, 12
Polar lows 12
Poriaz 56
precipitation 5
pressure conversions 6
pressure rises 42
Pyr 54

ridges 12
Riesenburg 54
ring haloes 18-19
Roeteturm 54

Saffir-Simpson Scale 28
Samiel 54
Santa Ana 54
satellite image of Earth and Moon 57, 58
Scirroco 56
sea breezes 8
sea, freezing 52, 53
seiches 15
Sharav 56
sheet lightning 26
single cell storms 20
skiing hazards 46
sky-ray transmission 20
snowfalls 38, 39
snow-shadows 38
snowstorms 36-9
solar haloes 42
Southerly buster 57
Southern Hemisphere winds 8
Southern Oscillation 58
speed conversions 6
Steppenwind 56
storm cells 21
storm indicators 18
storm surges 15, 28
stratocumulus 6

stratus 6
strong breeze 13
Suhaili 56
sunburn 62
supercells 20
Surazo 54

Tehuantepecer 57
temperature conversion 6
thunder 20
thunderstorms 20-3, 25
tornadoes 9-10, 20, 32-5
trade winds 7
Tramontana 54
tropical depressions 28
tropical revolving storms 9-10, 28, 30
tropical storms 30
    preparation for 31
tropopause 6
troposphere 6
troughs 11
tsunamis 15
typhoons 10, 28, 30

UV Index 62

valley winds 40
Vaudaire 54
Vent d'Espagne 54

water vapour 9
waterspouts 32-5, 47
weather map 11
willy-willies 28, 57
wind 7-8
    chill 50
    force 13
    speeds 9
    storms 16-19
    strong 13
Wisper 56

64